THE SARAWAK CHINESE

THE SARAWAK CHINESE

JOHN M. CHIN

KUALA LUMPUR
OXFORD UNIVERSITY PRESS
OXFORD NEW YORK MELBOURNE
1981

Oxford University Press
OXFORD LONDON GLASGOW
NEW YORK TORONTO MELBOURNE WELLINGTON
KUALA LUMPUR SINGAPORE HONG KONG TOKYO
DELHI BOMBAY CALCUTTA MADRAS KARACHI
NAIROBI DAR ES SALAAM CAPE TOWN

ISBN 0 19 580470 8

*Printed in Malaysia by Sun U Book Co. Sdn. Bhd., Kuala Lumpur
Published by Oxford University Press, 3, Jalan 13/3,
Petaling Jaya, Selangor, Malaysia*

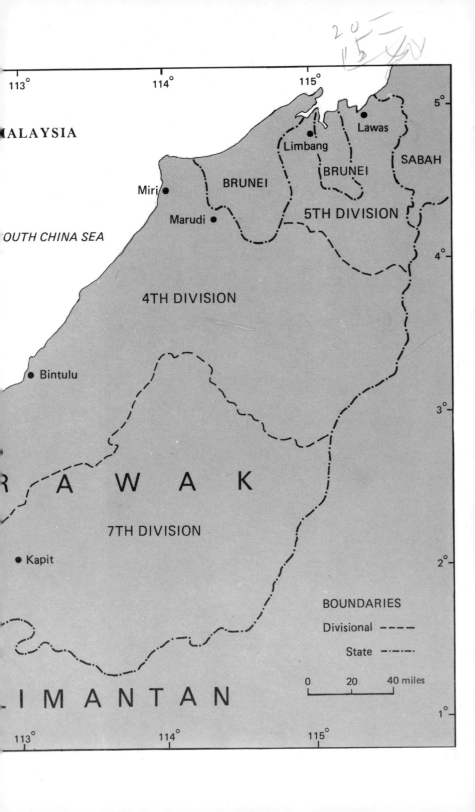

Foreword

I would like to commend Mr John M. Chin on his book *The Sarawak Chinese*. Obviously Mr Chin has devoted a good deal of time in doing research on the history of the Chinese in Sarawak. Much of this information which he has managed to collect together came from old publications, but most of the information had to be obtained from people whose families have long associations with Sarawak.

The book should be a very useful source of information to those who are interested in the important role which the Chinese in Sarawak have played in the development of the State.

I hope that Mr Chin's efforts would encourage other students of history to delve further into the past and make a greater in-depth study on the subject as there are obviously some gaps which need to be filled.

The inclusion in the book of various references which Mr Chin has made to some of the earlier works on Sarawak should prove useful for those who wish to pursue a study of the rather interesting and in some ways romantic past history of Sarawak.

Mr Chin has made a very important contribution to knowledge of the State and I recommend the book to all those who are interested in the future development of the State for it is

only by looking at the past that one can obtain a better perspective of the present and foster better understanding among
our multi-racial society.

Tan Sri Datuk Ong Kee Hui
P.M.N., P.N.B.S., P.G.D.K., M.P.
Kementerian Sains, Teknologi
dan Alam Sekitar, Malaysia

Preface

WRITERS of South-East Asian history are apt to treat the presence of Chinese people in Borneo in the early centuries, including their presence in what is now known as Sarawak and Sabah, as part of a larger exodus into the South Seas or *nanyang*, a collective term applied by the Chinese to the territories of South-East Asia, more specifically the Malay Archipelago, to which their compatriots have migrated. The process of Chinese emigration began, not as a planned campaign to establish colonies or create permanent communities overseas, but as a gradual penetration following sporadic trade and political contacts made over many centuries. Occasionally this was done with the cognizance of the Imperial dynasties but more often on the initiative, in the face of official bans, of enterprising merchants, daring seafarers, and other intrepid adventurers who lived on China's south and east coasts which are indented with many fine bays and harbours. Several historical factors stimulated this emigration: unrelieved population pressure on arid and unproductive land, contiguity of the coastal provinces of South China to South-East Asia, and political unrest and turmoil on the Chinese mainland. The emigrants came almost exclusively from the southern provinces of Kwangtung, Fukien and, to a lesser extent, Kiangsu.

If the Chinese presence in Borneo was treated by historians as part of the *nanyang* story, in Sarawak itself it was merely regarded as incidental to the saga of a State created as a separate political entity by the rule of the Brooke Rajahs. Historical accounts of the past invariably included the Sarawak Chinese together with the other ethnic groups who have given the country its distinctive multi-racial character.

Such treatment of the Chinese is easy to understand. Geographically Sarawak is part of Borneo; politically the State did not exist until Brooke rule began in 1841. Although a few Chinese lived in the border areas between Sarawak and West Borneo long before Brunei gave up its suzerainty over the country, it was the orderly development of the Brooke regime that subsequently attracted large-scale Chinese settlement.

The emergence of Sarawak as an independent state within Malaysia since 1963 has once more focused world-wide attention on this one-time exotic eastern kingdom ruled for a century by autocratic Europeans. The revived interest in Sarawak, particularly in the ethnic origins, cultures, and customs of its peoples of many races is reflected by increased curiosity about Sarawak's Chinese community which accounts for one-third of the country's total population and whose contribution to its social, economic, and political life has been largely responsible for the State's growth and development.

This book examines chosen aspects of that community's social and economic organization and its historical, cultural and educational developments over the years from the Chinese perspective, and covers the period from the early Chinese settlers in the gold fields of West Borneo down to the present well-ordered and prosperous society. It is written primarily for the general reader but it also aims to serve as a basic introduction to more detailed studies on the subject by other researchers.

In the preparation of this work I am indebted to many. Foremost on my list are the illustrious authors of various nationalities, past and present, whose works I have consulted and who have provided me with both the inspiration and the background material. Since any expression of my gratitude by merely including their works in the bibliography would be inadequate I wish to acknowledge here my indebtedness to them. My special thanks are due to Tan Sri Datuk Ong Kee Hui, P.M.N., P.N.B.S., P.G.D.K., M.P., Federal Minister of Science, Technology and Environment, for his encouragement and for consenting to write the Foreword; to the Sarawak Museum for the use of the facilities in its archives; to Mr Lucas Chin, P.B.S., Curator, and Mr Loh Chee Jin, Archivist, for their helpful suggestions and assistance; and finally to the Sarawak Museum and the Borneo Literature Bureau (now Dewan Bahasa dan Pustaka, Cawangan Sarawak) for making available a number of maps and photographs used in the illustrations.

Kuching   JOHN M. CHIN
1979

Contents

Foreword		v
Preface		vii
Maps		xiii
Plates		xiv
1.	EARLY HISTORY: CHINESE PRESENCE AND TRADE	1
	Early Chinese Contacts with Borneo	1
	Contacts with Sarawak	9
2.	EARLY SOCIAL AND POLITICAL ORGANIZATION: THE KONGSI SYSTEM	13
	Social and Political Organization	13
	Lan-fang Kongsi	18
3.	THE END OF KONGSI RULE AND MIGRATION TO SARAWAK	22
	Kongsi Wars and the Dutch Conquest	22
	Border Migration and Bau Kongsi	25
4.	THE CHINESE REBELLION, 1857	27
	Pre-Rebellion Events and the Triad Society	27
	The Rebellion, Occupation of Kuching, and Defeat	34
5.	POST-REBELLION CHINESE PIONEERS	40
	Early Pioneers	40
	Extension of Sarawak's Territory	48

6. CHINESE IMMIGRATION AND DEVELOPMENT OF
   AGRICULTURE, 1863–1941   51
   Chinese Immigrants: Recruited, Free, and
       Sponsored Groups   51
   Agricultural Settlements in First, Third, and
       Other Divisions   59

7. PRE-WAR SOCIAL AND ECONOMIC ORGANIZATION   71
   Economic Power and Leadership Structure   71
   Communal Organization: the Establishment of
       Temples, Associations, and Schools   80
   Role of Education with a Perspective of Chinese
       and English Educational Systems   84

8. THE JAPANESE OCCUPATION AND AFTER   95
   The Japanese Occupation   95
   Early Post-war Years and Colonial Rule   101

9. CHINESE IN PARTY POLITICS   117
   The Formation of Parties   117
   Chinese Participation in Government   123
   Conclusion   131

   Appendixes   136
   Bibliography   143
   Index   148

Maps

Sarawak in Malaysia   *front endpaper*
The Growth of Sarawak   *back endpaper*
1. Borneo *c.*1839   *facing page* 1
2. Lan-fang and Montrado Kongsis in West
   Borneo (nineteenth century)   12
3. Distribution of Chinese Population   52

Plates

Between pages 48 and 49

1. Early T'ang Ewer Excavated at Santubong, 1956 (Courtesy Sarawak Museum)

2. Chinese Goldminers, Bau (from *Old Sarawak—A Pictorial Study*, Craig A. Lockard & Graham E. Saunders, Kuching, Borneo Literature Bureau; now Dewan Bahasa dan Pustaka, Cawangan Sarawak)

3. Sarawak River and Kuching Town, 1839 (from *Kuching, Past and Present*, Elizabeth Pollard, Kuching, Borneo Literature Bureau; now Dewan Bahasa dan Pustaka, Cawangan Sarawak)

4. Chinese Shops along Main Bazaar, 1880 (from *Old Sarawak—A Pictorial Study*, Craig A. Lockard & Graham E. Saunders, Kuching, Borneo Literature Bureau; now Dewan Bahasa dan Pustaka, Cawangan Sarawak)

5. Ong Ewe Hai (from *Old Sarawak—A Pictorial Study*, Craig A. Lockard & Graham E. Saunders, Kuching, Borneo Literature Bureau; now Dewan Bahasa dan Pustaka, Cawangan Sarawak)

6. Law Kian Huat (from *Old Sarawak—A Pictorial Study*, Craig A. Lockard & Graham E. Saunders, Kuching, Borneo Literature Bureau; now Dewan Bahasa dan Pustaka, Cawangan Sarawak)

7. Wong Nai Siong, Sketch from an Old Photograph (Courtesy Dewan Bahasa dan Pustaka, Cawangan Sarawak)

8. Ong Tiang Swee (from *Kuching, Past and Present*, Elizabeth Pollard, Kuching, Borneo Literature Bureau; now Dewan Bahasa dan Pustaka, Cawangan Sarawak)

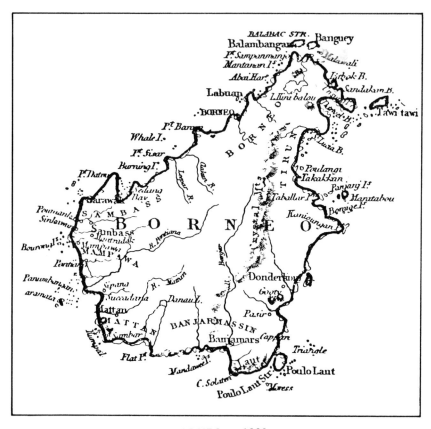

1. BORNEO c. 1839

1

Early History:
Chinese Presence and Trade

EARLY CHINESE CONTACTS WITH BORNEO

LYING across the equator at the geographic centre of South-East Asia, Borneo, the world's third largest island, has since early times enjoyed contacts with its island neighbours and with the ancient kingdoms on the Asian continent. Its contacts with China were via old-established sea-routes and were made possible by the navigational knowledge and ship-building skill of the Chinese. The focal point of contact was the old kingdom of P'oli (婆利) or P'olo (婆羅), known from the T'ang (唐) dynasty (618–907) onwards more specifically as P'oni (浡泥), which is believed to be an older name for Bruni or Brunei. Fan Tsuo (樊綽), writing in his book on the 'Barbarians' at the close of the T'ang dynasty, describes P'oni as a kingdom in the South Seas. P'oni at the height of its power comprised fourteen provinces, covering the entire northern coast of Borneo and extending as far as the present southern Philippines.

Early in the fifth century the high-ranking Chinese Buddhist monk Fa Hsien (法顯·) stopped in Ye-p'o-ti (耶婆提), on his return journey by sea from India after a pilgrimage. Braddell, writing about this event, believes that Ye-p'o-ti was in

Borneo while other writers such as Hall maintain that Fa Hsien probably visited Sumatra or Java after calling at Ceylon. In the official Chinese chronicles P'oli was first mentioned in the Liang (梁) dynasty (502–566), followed by Sui (隋) (589–618) and T'ang. All three dynasties left records indicating that P'oli sent tribute to China—in 517, 522, 616, 630 and 699. Another early Chinese source gives an interesting location of P'oni that it was on an island to the south-east of Cambodia, two months' journey by sea travelling south-east from Canton. The journey thither was made by way of the Malay Peninsula. As Java and Sumatra lie farther south than Borneo from Cambodia and Canton, the description seems to fit Borneo better. The same source also mentions that the people of P'oni were skilled in throwing a chiselled knife edged like a saw, and in the use of weapons similar to those of the Chinese; that they punished a murderer or thief by cutting off the offender's hands, and that part of their custom was to offer sacrifices to the spirits when there was no moon, the sacrifice being placed in bowls to float away on the water. They wove two types of cotton cloth called *kupa* and *tieh* from a local cotton plant. All the particulars given with regard to the people of P'oni were true of one or other of the Bornean races living in or near Brunei. The chiselled knife was known to have been used there formerly. The cutting off of the hands of a murderer or thief was a favourite form of punishment in Brunei until recent times. The Kadayans offered sacrifices after each new moon. The Melanaus in Sarawak used to set laden rafts afloat on the rivers to propitiate the spirits of the sea. *Kupa*, probably a Chinese corruption of *kapok* is a well-known Malay word for cotton and *taya* is a common name for cotton among some of Sarawak's native tribes.

P'oni continued to send tribute to China during the Sung (宋) dynasty (960–1279). The Sung historian Chao Ju-kua (趙汝适) gives a detailed account of P'oni's trade relations with China in his *Chu Fan Chi* (諸蕃志), or *Record of Foreign Lands*, written about 1225. He states that P'oni was a powerful, civilized kingdom

... whose city walls are built of timber. . . . P'oni has a population of more than 10,000; it has control over 14 provinces. The king's palace is magnificently built and thatched. . . . In the second year of T'ai Ping (1082) P'oni again sent tribute to the Son of Heaven. . . . P'oni is in sea trade with the Middle Kingdom and Arabia. Whenever Chinese sailing vessels arrive at P'oni the masters are wont to present the king with choice Chinese food and drink. For this purpose Chinese vessels plying between P'oni and China always carry one or two highly-skilled cooks. . . .

The Mongols under Genghiz Khan ended the Sung reign in 1276 and established the Yuan (元) dynasty (1276–1368). Overseas contact was far less important as the first two emperors, Genghiz Khan and Ogotai, were bent on conquest and subjugation. It was not until after Kublai Khan became master of all China in 1280 that he undertook further military campaigns in East and South-East Asia. In 1292 he sent an expedition under General Su P'e (史弼) to subdue the powerful and ambitious Singhasari king, Kertanagara, who ruled in Java. However, when the expedition arrived, Kertanagara had already been slain. Vijaya, his son-in-law, established with Chinese help a new kingdom at Majapahit which in time succeeded Srivijaya, extending its rule over Sumatra (Palembang), Bali, Timor, Ternate, Luzon, and the northern coasts of Borneo, including Brunei and Sulu. This Hindu-Javan kingdom of Majapahit in turn fell to the Muslim Malays around 1475 and with its fall Brunei came under Malay domination and Islamic influence. Recording the Chinese (Mongol) expedition to Java the official chronicles of Kublai Khan mentioned that on its voyage to Java the expedition called at Karimata and Galam, two places situated on the west coast of Borneo. It has since been suggested that part of the expedition landed in the northern part of Borneo (the present Sabah) and left behind a Chinese settlement which extended to the Sulu Islands.

The Yuan dynasty, for all its conquests, lasted barely one hundred years. In 1368 Chu Hung Wu (朱洪武) seized control from the Mongols and re-established the Chinese dynasty of Ming (明) (1368–1643). One of his first acts was to develop a navy consisting of ocean-going vessels, heavily-armed and well-equipped for long voyages, to be used as an instrument of trade and national power. Chu Hung Wu was a southern Chinese and established his capital at Nanking. He sent envoys to Central Asia to keep watch over the Turko-Mongol emperor, Tamerlane, whose dominions still threatened China's western borders, but he also sent his fleet out to the South Seas, to Sumatra and Borneo, and to Chola in Southern India, to make diplomatic and commercial contacts. As a result of these efforts during the next decade or so a number of East Indian trade embassies were established. However, tribute missions to China appeared to have declined towards the end of the fourteenth century. Ming annals related that in order to reinforce China's prestige Chu Hung Wu had, in the first years of his reign, 'to despatch an expedition to invade P'oni, a land lying close to Sulu and Java. The expedition after achieving much success was withdrawn. . . .'[1]

Perhaps the best account of the Chinese presence in Brunei is the story of Ong Sum Ping (王森屏), a Ming envoy and local governor. Ong Sum Ping settled with his followers on the Kinabatangan, a river on the east coast of present Sabah. There are no details of how he obtained his governorship, although it was likely that he succeeded to the appointment. If so, he might have been descended from those Chinese left behind by earlier expeditions. Ong Sum Ping's debut into history occurred around 1375. By the marriage of his daughter to the second sultan of Brunei, Sultan Akhmed, whose daughter in turn married Sharif Ali, an Arab who succeeded to the Brunei throne as Sultan Berkat, Ong Sum Ping became the forebear of a long line of Brunei sultans. The Sulu islanders, on the other hand, have a tradition that their first ruling sultan was a Fukien Chinese named Tan (陳).

Chinese contacts with *nanyang* were renewed and strengthened early in the fifteenth century during the reign of the third Ming emperor, Yung Lo (永樂), by the spectacular voyages of the imperial eunuch, Cheng Ho (鄭和).[2] Between 1405 and 1433 he made seven voyages, each in an armada of more than sixty ships, first to the Western Seas, an expression then in use for places west of Malacca, and then to the Indian Ocean, proceeding as far as Arabia and the East African coasts.

The ocean voyages were made possible because of China's old seafaring tradition. With a coastline stretching some 6,000 miles and dotted with many fine harbours and thousands of off-shore islands acting as natural breakwaters, China had been able, since medieval times,[3] to develop such cities as Canton in Kwangtung, Yangchow in Kiangsu, and Chuanchow in Fukien as centres of foreign trade, while Shanghai, Kanpu, Hangchow, and Ningpo were ports of growing importance. The invention of the compass contributed to China's navigational skill and the shipbuilding industry. By the twelfth century the geographical writer, Chou Chu-fei, was referring to China's ships plying the Southern Seas as 'huge hulls with sails like clouds, and each ship was carrying a year's supply of grain and hundreds of people'.

During his voyages Cheng Ho is said to have passed Borneo twice although it is not known if he actually called there. That some of his ships with his men on board did so seems to be of little doubt. Evidence of this is indicated by the fact that in 1405 the year of his first voyage, Maraja Kali, the King of P'oni sent tribute to the Ming court. This would appear to be the first recorded tribute from P'oni to China after 1082. Ming annals describe how the emperor, to show his magnanimity, conferred on Maraja Kali the official title of the King of P'oni, complete with the imperial seal and writ of appointment. So pleased was the king that he decided to visit the great country himself three years later, taking with him his wife and his son and heir. Maraja Kali died in Nanking, the Ming capital, before he could return to P'oni and was buried with royal honours on Stone Hill (石子岡) outside the capital city. His grave can still be located on Chep'o Hill (聚寶山) beyond the Chung Hua Gate in present-day Nanking. His son Hiawang (Si Awang) was then made king by the Chinese and sailed for home with his mother in 1411. There is evidence that Hiawang revisited China on several occasions and continued to send tribute.

Cheng Ho's voyages, officially sponsored by the Ming emperor, Yung Lo, resulted in Malacca being used as a midway base where warehouses were built to store money and provisions and where China-bound ships called to reprovision or to await the arrival of favourable winds for their onward journey to China. Because of the short distance between Malacca and Borneo and the sea-traffic that had been carried on between them from early times, it is safe to assume that this traffic increased after Cheng Ho's voyages—a traffic largely carried on by Chinese merchants in their junks. It was the practice of these merchants, before their trading ships sailed for China, to leave behind a small number of their crew as hostages of goodwill and to ensure their return. As the trading voyages increased so did the number of hostages left behind to form new Chinese settlements.

Although Cheng Ho's voyages to the *nanyang* were soon discontinued as the Emperor's advisers considered them to be wasteful and unnecessary, they nevertheless wrote a brilliant page in China's maritime history never equalled before or since. After these voyages, envoys from different overseas countries came to China to pay court, and trade embassies were set up which benefited both sides. Subsequently, too, more and more Chinese made their way to the South Seas, including Borneo, to trade and settle.

The Manchus defeated the Ming emperors and ruled China for nearly three hundred years as the Ch'ing (清) dynasty (1644–1911). Like the Mongols, they were foreign conquerors and their rule was resented by the Chinese. For the first hundred years of Ch'ing rule, the history of China was marked by a series of internal struggles among the Manchu ruling houses for power, of resistance movements and rebellions by the people to overthrow the Ch'ing and restore the Ming, and of military expeditions to subdue the border vassal states such as Annam (Indo-China) and Burma. The Manchus' policy was to pacify and unify China whose people's culture and language they in time assimilated, while keeping China isolated from the outside world. Overseas trade was not encouraged; emigration from China was prohibited by Imperial decree and until 1860 any one who left the country was liable to capital punishment.

Trade contact with the West was forced on China in the late seventeenth century, and by the nineteenth century a weakening dynasty had been compelled to open its seaports and assign free trade areas to the foreign powers that had defeated the Manchu forces. In 1860 the Treaty of Peking was signed with Britain, France, and Russia. One clause of the Treaty stipulated that all Chinese were in future at liberty to enter into service in the British colonies and other places overseas. This clause abrogated the Imperial ban on emigration. In consequence cheap Chinese labour on contract became available through coolie or labour brokers who set up business in the treaty ports. This labour was destined for service in the developing rubber plantations and tin mines of Java and the Straits Settlements, the sugar plantations of Cuba and West Indies, and the gold mines and railways of California. Conceivably a portion of this labour force found its way to the Borneo territories.

Early references to Chinese commerce and settlement in Borneo were made by Western writers, somewhat vaguely, from the sixteenth century onwards. According to Hunt a large Chinese settlement had existed on the shores of Borneo around 1520. Pigafetta, writing of Ferdinand Magellan's call at Brunei in 1521, did not mention such a settlement although it could have existed elsewhere on the Bornean coast. Pigafetta did, however, observe that Brunei officials of the Sultan's court were mounted on caparisoned elephants and were attired in magnificent Chinese silks. He also commented on the Chinese coinage and Chinese weights and measures in use there. Spenser St. John declared that in the early sixteenth century some Chinese had settled in Brunei and were engaged in those branches of industry in which they excelled. Hugh Low in 1848 noted that whereas at the time of Pigafetta's visit Brunei's population was estimated at 100,000, it had been reduced to 40,000 some two hundred years later, and of this

30,000 were Chinese who were mainly engaged in pepper cultivation. If Hugh Low was correct there had been a large population of Chinese settled in Brunei as early as the sixteenth and as late as the second half of the eighteenth century, and their industry had supplied Brunei with the main commodity for foreign trade. Until the entry of colonial powers such as the Portuguese, the Spanish, and the Dutch from the beginning of the sixteenth century, direct trade with Brunei was entirely in Chinese hands. This trade dwindled and eventually died out completely during the two centuries that followed, owing to fierce competition from the European powers. With it Chinese immigration into Brunei also ceased.

Reporting on this in 1863 St. John observed that at the time there were scarcely any Chinese left in Brunei's capital. Baring-Gould and Bampfylde describe the subsequent scene in Brunei and the passing of the Chinese junk trade in these words:

> On the picturesque hills that surround the town are still to be found traces of thriving plantations which formerly existed there and which extended for many miles into the interior. These have totally disappeared, with the population which cultivated them. In 1291, two centuries before the first European vessel rounded the Cape, Ser Marco Polo visited the Archipelago. He gives us the first narrative we possess of the Chinese junk trade to the west, and mentions a great and profitable traffic carried on by the Chinese with Borneo and this trade throve for many years afterwards; even in 1776 the commerce with China was considerable, though then it must have been declining, for it had ceased before the close of that century. Hunt records that in his time (1812) there were still to be seen at Brunei old docks capable of berthing vessels of from 500 to 600 tons. Now the most striking feature of the place is its profound poverty.[4]

In West Borneo trade between the Chinese and the Sultanates of Banjermasin, Pontianak, and Sambas began after the discovery of gold deposits in early times. This trade became so firmly established that in spite of constant efforts by the Dutch to dissuade the Borneo sultans from selling pepper to the Chinese, it was many years before they succeeded and an effective agreement was signed between the Dutch East India Company and the sultans.

CONTACTS WITH SARAWAK

There is no recorded evidence of direct early contacts between China and what is now Sarawak. Indications of an early Chinese presence were suggested by surface finds of Chinese coins, pottery sherds, and Venetian beads. These were said to have been Chinese trade goods, and were found at Santubong, a fishing village situated at the mouth of the Sarawak River near Kuching, in the last decade of the nineteenth century. The Chinese coins dated from the T'ang period onwards. Similar indications of a Chinese presence in early times may be seen in place names of distinctive Chinese flavour in the Sarawak delta area, of which Santubong (山都望), Bongkisam (黃紀三), Tanjong Sipang (四彭) and Pulau Satang (三唐) are examples.

Systematic excavations of half a dozen sites in the delta country (Santubong area) were carried out by the Sarawak Museum between 1947 and 1961, and the resultant unearthing of thousands of pottery and stoneware sherds, iron slugs, crucibles, coins, and other artefacts showed that Santubong and its surrounding areas formed a flourishing settlement and depôt for the Chinese junk trade in this part of Borneo. This trade seems to have begun in the T'ang era, and continued through the Sung and on to the Yuan dynasties, spanning roughly the period between 618 and 1368. From these extensive excavations it was discovered that at least two trade centres had existed in the Santubong area: one at Sungei Ja'ong about two miles from the present Santubong village, which existed in the T'ang and the early Sung eras; the other at Bongkisam, behind Santubong village, which was in use during the Sung and part of the Yuan dynasties (about 1000 to 1340). Two Chinese cemeteries were also found: Tanjong Kubu, a proletarian burial ground on a small headland half a mile west of Santubong and Tanjong Tegok, a burial ground for 'aristocrats', situated about half a mile from Santubong but to the east. The two cemeteries are believed to date from the T'ang period and were contemporaneous. Iron foundries were discovered in the excavation sites at Sungei Ja'ong, Sungei Buah, and Telok Sabang, together with quantities of iron slugs, crucibles, and remains of charcoal used in smelting. The extent of the iron workings and size of the iron slugs lying *in situ* lend support to the theory that the delta area was once the centre of an ancient but extensive iron industry worked either by the Chinese or on their orders, for use in weaponry or ship's stores or as a valuable trade commodity.

Ceramic dating established that nearly all the stoneware excavated in the Santubong area is certainly of Chinese origin, and that it was all made during the period T'ang-Sung-Yuan. The results of ceramic dating were substantiated in 1966 by radio-carbon testing carried out on some uncontaminated charcoal excavated at the Bongkisam site. The C-14 test showed that the charcoal sample dated from about 1315.[5] The conclusion is that the whole of the Sarawak River delta was an important site for Chinese trade at an early period, although there was no evidence of a permanent Chinese settlement there at the time. All activities in the delta area would appear to have ceased suddenly before 1370 or in the first years of the Ming period. This suggests that the early Ming emperors deliberately disrupted Chinese trading patterns in South-East Asia in an attempt to discourage private trading and to enforce the tribute system. In any event, all indications of Chinese presence in the Sarawak part of Borneo ended in the middle of the fifteenth century although they continued for a further hundred years or more in Brunei.

1. Ascribed to Ming Annals, Volume 225, section on Sulu.

2. Cheng Ho (also known as Sam Po) was in modern parlance a naturalized Chinese. He was a member of the Semur minority tribe that had settled in Kunyang, Yunnan, after his forebears had migrated from Central Asia, following the Mongol conquest. His family had embraced Islam and like many Chinese Muslims living in China's border provinces had assumed the Chinese surname of Ma (馬). The name Cheng Ho was given by Prince Yan (later Emperor Yung Lo) when he entered the

latter's service as a eunuch. See John Gittings, *A Chinese View of China* (B.B.C., London, 1963).

3. Some Chinese records state that Emperor Wu Ti (武帝) of the Western Han (206 B.C.–A.D. 24) had sent a mission by sea to southern India as early as the second century B.C.

4. S. Baring-Gould and C. A. Bampfylde, *History of Sarawak under its Two White Rajahs* (London, 1909), p. 44.

5. See T. Harrisson and Stanley J. O'Connor, *Excavations of the Prehistoric Iron Industry in West Borneo*, Vol. I, Data Paper No. 72, Southeast Asia Programme, Cornell University (New York, 1969); also *Sarawak, 1962: Annual Report of Sarawak Government*, Part III, History.

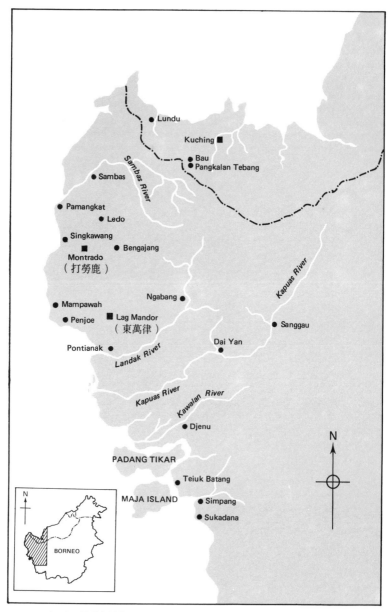

2. LAN-FANG AND MONTRADO KONGSIS IN WEST
BORNEO (NINETEENTH CENTURY)

2
Early Social and Political Organization: The Kongsi System

SOCIAL AND POLITICAL ORGANIZATION

EARLY Chinese records show that from the sixth century onwards sea-traffic linked China with Borneo, but it was not until the middle of the eighteenth century that large numbers of Chinese settlers arrived in West Borneo, lured by the gold rush and the establishment of gold mines, such as that opened by the Sultan of Sambas at Larak in 1750. An examination of the tombstones erected to Chinese immigrants buried at Mempawa and Mandor showed the earliest date to be 1745.[1] Massive Chinese presence in West Borneo in the later centuries is also attested by accounts of Dutch attempts, from the seventeenth century, to gain control of the pepper trade, which was mainly in the hands of Chinese.

The Chinese settlers in West Borneo consisted of two main groups: descendants of those who had come with past military expeditions or trade voyages and who were left behind as hostages of goodwill, being Chinese of mixed blood whose mothers were native women; and immigrants from the coastal districts in the two provinces of Kwangtung and Fukien in Southern China, who in spite of the Imperial ban, lifted only after the 1860 Treaty, had left China in search of a better life overseas. It was estimated that until 1823, when the Dutch took over West Borneo, there was an annual intake of 3,000 new arrivals from China.[2]

The pioneers endured great hardship in the early years, as may be seen from the following account related by two Dutchmen, de Groot and Schlegedate, who arrived at the court of Sultan Omar Alamudin in Pontianak in 1772.

> The Chinese [who] were pale and exhausted by the misery of the long and difficult crossing of the sea, directed their steps humbly towards the Sultan's palace and threw themselves on his magnanimity, praying for the grant of a small portion of his territory where they might settle.[3]

The story goes that their humble petition was answered and they were assigned to the district of Larak where they settled. It is clear that the Chinese immigrants to West Borneo had no territorial ambitions. They came to look for a fortune in gold; or, failing this, for a concession of land on which they could grow pepper and food crops. They were thus ready to make obeisance to the local sultan or any other ruler.

As their numbers increased the immigrants soon spread out. From the coastal towns of Sambas, Pontianak, and Mempawa they penetrated into the interior of Montrado (打勞鹿), Lag Mandor (東萬律), Buna, Sekanda, and Sintang. By the nineteenth century it was variously estimated that as few as 31,000 and as many as 150,000 Chinese settlers were living in West Borneo, of whom about 90,000 were engaged in the gold region.[4]

The chief occupation of the West Borneo Chinese at that time was gold mining. Gold had been discovered in the region and worked since ancient times. The rest of the population was involved in agriculture. Trading and other essential services also began to flourish as gold mining grew from individual ventures to corporate mines operated by Chinese kongsis employing thousands of labourers. Both for the miners in kongsi employ and individual immigrants who struck out for themselves, agriculture was of basic importance. All immigrants from China came from an agricultural background, especially the Hakkas who almost exclusively formed the total population of the mining region. The same could still be said of the local-born Chinese of mixed racial origin. Their first concern was an adequate food supply. Before a new arrival worked on his own or decided to join the kongsi, he usually planted all kinds of food crops on any vacant land he could find or rent. The more enterprising would cultivate trade crops such as pepper or gambier for which there was a steady demand. It was the policy of Chinese mining kongsis to encourage their workers to clear and cultivate mining concession land, not actually in use for gold prospecting, for the cultivation of food and cash crops which not only ensured self-sufficiency for the miners but also provided additional revenue for the kongsis. The tradesmen were either ex-miners or those brought in by the kongsis to supply essential services.

At this point it is relevant to digress from the main narrative to explain more fully the Chinese kongsi system which the West Borneo miners organized and maintained for more than a hundred years, and to discuss its origin, object, social and political organization, and power structure. Such an exposé is necessary if we are to understand the historical events that led to its continuity among the Chinese goldminers living in Upper Sarawak before their rebellion against James Brooke's rule, and the effect this rebellion had on the structure of Chinese society in Sarawak.

The kongsi system had its roots in the village organization of South China and was ingrained in the Chinese social structure. Barbara Ward, writing about the Hakka kongsi system in Borneo, points out that those who saw it as something apart, without recognizing its connection with the basic Chinese social structure and with the historical and geographical environment in which it had developed, tended either to see the kongsi as a secret society conspiring against all regular civil government or as a prototype of modern republican democracy. She considers both views misconceived, as the kongsi system was in reality the natural outcome of the experience of Chinese immigrants who had come to a strange land in compact clan and village groups, and who had to find ways to secure their livelihood, self-protection, and governance.[5]

The Chinese immigrants came to West Borneo as peaceful people whose sole reason for settling in a strange land was to seek a better life for themselves and their families and kindred in China. They were therefore anxious to show respect to local rulers with whom they always strove to enter into agreements to obtain mining and agricultural concessions for which they paid taxes in one form or another, and to whom they were ready to pledge allegiance. However, they lived in troublous times, and soon discovered that their local liege lords could afford them little protection as they had to contend with native tribes rebelling against their rule. The Dutch colonialists made increasing encroachments on their territories and the sultans were soon powerless even to protect themselves. To safeguard their mining rights and their land concessions large groups of miners and settlers formed themselves into kongsis (公司) or communal partnerships, so that people sharing the same economic interests, braving the same hazards and pursuing the same socio-political goals should band together in order to govern themselves and conduct their own affairs. The kongsis were therefore self-governing communities, regulated by their own laws and having their own machinery for enforcement. They also provided social and educational services for their members, meted out justice through a judicial system, and employed a peace-keeping force. They enjoyed an autonomous status recognized or at least accepted by the local sultans.

As more mines were developed the kongsis also increased their power and influence. The larger kongsis were often in a position to assist their local suzerains in putting down rebellions. There is evidence that some kongsis in time grew so powerful that they placed the local rulers under their tutelage. This they did primarily to ensure the stability of these rulers, an essential for continual peaceful settlement, rather than with the object of creating a new nation in the Bornean wilderness. Only Lo Fang-pai (羅芳伯), founder of the Lan-fang kongsi (蘭芳公司), had visions of his kongsi becoming an outpost of the Middle Kingdom, an ambition he was in fact never able to realize, as he failed to establish a colonial connection with China. All the other kongsis, including its powerful rival, Ta-kong (大港),[6] which fought the Dutch for many years, maintained their status quo, content with the relationship already established with the local rulers.

Because the West Borneo kongsis were composed almost entirely of people from four of the Hakka-speaking districts in the Kwangtung province: Kiaying (嘉應), now Mei Hsien (梅縣), Tap'u (大埔), Kityang (揭陽) or Hoppo (河婆), and Huilai (惠來) or Hailu-feng (海陸豐), they were all organized in the same way. These four districts are situated close to each other and each uses a variant of Hakka, but together with others speaking Cantonese, Teochew, Hainanese, Luichew dialects, and other variations of Hakka (such as Sin Ann or Huichow) they form one Kwangtung province, and its inhabitants are collectively known as *Kwangtung-ren* (廣東人). As the kongsi members came to Borneo in clan groups linked together by blood affinity or surname bond, it became natural for them all to adopt similar methods of traditional village organization, long in use in China, for building up their own organizations, but with adaptations to suit the new conditions. This similarity of kongsi organization in Borneo was observed by Earl as early as 1834 and has been referred to by other writers.

To understand more fully the importance of the role Chinese kongsis played in the history of both West Borneo and Sarawak in the nineteenth century, let us look closely at the organization and administration of one of the largest kongsis, the Lan-fang, which had a life span of 108 years and, fortunately, had left a written account of its organization. This kongsi, unlike others, was founded by an intellectual, Lo Fang-pai, and throughout its existence it was able to attract to its service scholars as well as other gifted persons. The Lan-fang account was written by Yap Hsiang Yun[7] (葉祥雲), son-in-law of its last President. It was probably first mentioned by the Dutch-Sino scholar, de Groot, in his book on the Chinese kongsis in Borneo, *Het Kongsiwezen van Borneo*, which provided the basis for studies by later day scholars.

LAN-FANG KONGSI

The history of Lan-fang is the story of a dynasty. Because of its long life span and the similarity of its organization to other kongsis, Lan-fang is a typical example of all the Chinese kongsis in West Borneo during the eighteenth and nineteenth centuries.

Lo Fang-pai was a Kiaying Hakka born about 1736. He is said to have stayed at home to study the classics with a view to passing the Imperial examinations and obtaining an official appointment. Like other men of his time he was married at an early age and fathered a son. Frustrated in the realization of his scholastic ambitions and being influenced by many of his countrymen who were then leaving China to seek their fortunes in *nanyang* he decided to join his kinsmen and left home in 1772. He landed in the same year at a small town near Pontianak. For a while he became a school teacher for a living. He was soon lured, however, by the possibilities in gold mines in the neighbouring district of Sambas, and with the help of some friends he began prospecting for gold. Because of his scholarly background and his unusual organizing ability they soon made him their leader. He gathered around him a nucleus of trusted helpers whom he organized into a sworn brotherhood—the Brotherhood of Eighteen. In 1775 he and his followers seized the gold mine called Shan Hsin Gold Lake (山心金湖) in the Lag Mandor district of Sambas, which had been established some years before by Tap'u Hakkas under the leadership of one Chang Ah Chai (張亞才). The leader fled but Lo Fang-pai was able to persuade the remaining Tap'u gold miners to stay and help to work the mines. Lo Fang-pai developed Shan Hsin into the Lan-fang Kongsi. He installed a presidential system and set about building it up into one

of the largest autonomous communities of his time. He maintained good relations with the Sultan of Sambas and other
local rulers to whom his kongsi paid taxes. He gained great
renown by assisting the Sultan to suppress local rebellions.
His exploits, coupled with his prestige among his own people,
made him the undisputed leader in Lag Mandor. During the
next few years Lan-fang extended its jurisdiction by annexation over the whole of this part of Borneo. At the height of
its power Lan-fang's jurisdiction covered a large portion in
the south of the West Borneo territory, with the exception of
the Montrado kongsi, the Ta-kong. In 1777 Lan-fang boasted
of a population of 40,000 of whom about 20,000 were indigenous natives. Lo Fang-pai's Dayak wife played an able role
in recruiting natives into his fold.

During Lo Fang-pai's nineteen years of presidency, between
1775 and 1794, his official title was Ta T'ang Chung Chang
(大唐總長) or President of Great China. In diplomatic matters
he sometimes styled himself the King of Western Borneo. The
hopes he entertained of attaching his realm to the Chinese
empire were never fulfilled. He had capable military leaders
to help him to unite the people but there appeared to be no
statesmen of sufficient stature to share his administrative
tasks, though it was likely that he did not really wish to share
these with any one else. The picture that emerges from the
records is that of a man with a determined will who was an
absolute dictator throughout his life. And yet the Lan-fang
was more of a republic than a dictatorship as it possessed a
two-stage election system. Government was at the central and
provincial levels. At the central level, organization was un-
complicated. The capital was located in Lag Mandor. The
President and other important officials of the kongsi were
elected by the people according to a constitution which was
not written but was accepted by general consent. Their term
of office was not defined, but if they were considered incom-
petent or delinquent they could be impeached by the voters.
Under the President was a Vice-president, who was also the
Chief-of-Staff and lived in Salamon, a gold-mining district

nearby. The President had the right to recommend several candidates to succeed him. In the event of an election and installation of a successor to the office of President, the Vice-president would act as President. It is not known if the President worked with advisers.

Lo Fang-pai divided the areas under his jurisdiction into administrative districts called provinces which were then subdivided into prefectures and counties. Presiding over the prefecture was a magistrate and in the county a captain. Officials at provincial or district level were elected. The method of election is nowhere described, but de Groot points out that it was always the most influential—and usually the richest—men in the individual villages, and consequently men with obvious leadership qualities who were elected. The actual election was, by implication, done by nomination and public agreement, but this should not rule out direct appointments made by the charismatic head of the kongsi. The lesser officials served in a voluntary capacity and received little or no financial remuneration. Magistrates and captains were in charge of both judicial and administrative affairs although independent tribunals of justice also existed. Customs offices were set up to collect taxes, levy tolls, and deal with immigration.

The President or head of the kongsi consulted with the prefecture (district) and county (settlement) representatives, especially over issues of importance. The kongsi and district heads had powers to elect and depose lesser officials although they themselves derived their authority delegated from the settlement upward and not originating at the top. Within their own area elected officials maintained law and order and dealt with disputes and offences. Consultation in the settlements was with the family heads, and at the district and kongsi levels with the officials. Judgement on important cases had to be discussed with the kongsi head. Robbery, murder, and political crimes were tried by a tribunal composed of the kongsi head and other senior officials sitting in the kongsi house.

Lan-fang under Lo Fang-pai's administration became very prosperous. Plebiscites held over issues of local concern served as a stimulus to economic development. The gold mines were operated by the Lan-fang corporation, a state enterprise. Lan-fang set up its own arsenals to manufacture guns, cannons, and ammunition. There was a small contingent of men-at-arms to keep the peace in the kongsi. In the event of war conscription was imposed. Gold mining was not the only business of the Lan-fang. To supply food to the miners farm settlements around the mines were encouraged; and when the supply of gold dwindled in the later part of the nineteenth century the farm settlements came into their own with the breeding of domestic animals for home consumption and the kongsi markets. The exploitation of forest resources necessitated the building of roads and the maintenance of waterways. Officials were appointed to conduct religious worship and public ceremonies, and temples were also erected. Education, to which the Chinese gave the highest priority, was supported by the kongsi. Noted scholars were brought over from China to West Borneo to teach the Confucian classics.[8]

1. Reference Lo Hsiang-lin's *A Historical Survey of the Lan-fang Presidential System in Western Borneo by Lo Fang-pai and other Overseas Chinese* (羅香林著：西婆羅洲羅芳伯等所建共和國考。), Hong Kong, Institute of Chinese Culture, 1961, text in Chinese. Lo in turn made use of material recorded by de Groot, author of *Het Kongsiwezen van Borneo*.

2. G. W. Earl, *The Eastern Seas* (London, 1837).

3. Victor Purcell, *The Chinese of Southeast Asia* (Oxford University Press, 1965).

4. Earl, op. cit.

5. Barbara Ward, 'A Hakka Kongsi in Borneo', *Journal of Oriental Studies*, Hong Kong, Vol. 1, No. 2, July 1959.

6. It is interesting to note in passing that such names as Ta-kong (Tyquong in older accounts), Lo Fang-pai, Lan-fang kongsi, etc. have appeared in different romanized forms. Lo Fang-pai, and Lan-fang, for example, are in the Mandarin version. In the dialect used in the West Borneo kongsis, Hakka, they should read T'ai-kong, Lo Fong-pak, and Lan-fong Kongsi respectively.

7. Yap Siang Yun's 'Annals of Lan-fang Kongsi' (蘭芳公司歷代年冊) as quoted by Lo Hsiang-lin.

8. Lo Hsiang-lin, op. cit.

3

The End of Kongsi Rule and Migration to Sarawak

KONGSI WARS AND THE DUTCH CONQUEST

CHINESE kongsi dominance in West Borneo would undoubtedly have continued for many more years had it not been for interference from a foreign power, the Dutch. As early as 1600 Oliver van Noort, the Dutch trade representative, tried to enter the textile market in Borneo and visited Brunei to negotiate a trade agreement with the Sultan. His efforts failed because of Brunei's preference for Chinese linen and household goods. In the end he had to enlist the services of a Chinese middleman to achieve his purpose.

In order to expand their colonial activities in Borneo the Dutch formed the East India Company in 1602 and six years later set up a trade factory in Sambas. By 1611 the Dutch had firmly established themselves at Jakarta which they renamed Batavia. They then proceeded to drive the Portuguese out of their settlements. The power of the Portuguese had been weakened by the Spanish from the Philippines, and one by one their settlements, from Malacca to Java and Borneo, were taken from them. By the end of the century the Dutch were masters of the Malay Archipelago. They next turned their attention to the lucrative trade in spices and other native produce that China was conducting directly with Borneo and the neighbouring islands. Early attempts by the Company to negotiate trade agreements with the Sultans of Sambas, Santoh, Pontianak, Banjermasin, and Brunei had met with little success because the Chinese there were too well-entrenched in their trade connections with the Sultans. It was not until 1644 that the Dutch managed to secure contracts to purchase pepper from the Sultan of Banjermasin. Even so, the latter had insisted, as late as 1748, on reserving 50,000 pounds of pepper for the Chinese traders.

This competition in trade continued into the second half of the eighteenth century when the struggle for control was not confined to pepper and native produce but was extended to the more valuable commodity, gold, which the Chinese kongsis were mining from concessions at Sambas and Montrado, lying between Pontianak and Sambas. Harrisson and O'Connor report that by 1820 the Chinese kongsis had established no less than thirteen large and fifty-seven small mines, mostly in the area around Montrado, and that from this source alone gold production was double that of the whole of Sumatra.[1] The mines at Montrado were in the hands of the Ta-kong kongsi which by the beginning of the nineteenth century had eclipsed in importance its arch-rival, Lan-fang, as the latter had begun to decline owing to the inferior leadership of its later Presidents.

Since 1779 the Dutch East India Company had been attempting to enter into separate agreements with the Sultans of Pontianak, Mempawa, and Sambas for effective control of the Chinese mining kongsis on the ground that their government in Batavia now had jurisdiction over these territories. After the Dutch government in the Netherlands took over from the Company in 1799 these efforts were redoubled. Not unnaturally the Chinese viewed the Dutch attempts as an infringement of their kongsis' autonomy, a grave threat to their communal institution, to their livelihood, and to the free exercise of their liberties. They reacted at first by refusing to pay taxes, withholding co-operation from the Dutch and finally offering military resistance when further steps were taken to curtail their mining operations and trade ventures. The Dutch retaliated by sending punitive expeditions into the mining areas. Thus began the wars against the Chinese kongsis in 1802 which continued spasmodically for the next thirty-five years. Between 1811 and 1816 British colonial power was on the ascendancy and temporarily replaced the Dutch in Batavia. This short British interlude did not affect the supremacy of the kongsis in Borneo. But after the Treaty of Vienna in 1814 the Dutch regained the overlordship of the Archipelago and they resolved to establish absolute control over West Borneo. However, effective action was interrupted for a time by the Great Java War. In the interim Chinese kongsis continued to thrive although they were engaged from time to time in local warfare and strife among themselves. By 1850 the Dutch had gained complete control over the Sambas Sultanate and were ready to move against Ta-kong. The initial attacks were unsuccessful as Ta-kong was able to take advantage of familiar terrain and its strong fortifications to beat off the Dutch troops. Then Ta-kong decided to punish the San-Tiou-Kow kongsi (三條溝公司) which had sided with the Dutch. Ta-kong attacked its kongsi house situated in Seminis, near Pamangkat, in July 1850 and drove its people out of Seminis. Some escaped northwards, others fled to Pamangkat whence they sought assistance from the Dutch in Pontianak; yet others made their way across the Sambas River to find sanctuary with the Lan-fang people who had become allies of the Dutch, or to join their relatives and friends who had a few years earlier crossed the border to settle in Upper Sarawak. Ta-kong, on the trail of those fleeing to Pamangkat, promptly attacked them there before Dutch help could come and blew up their kongsi house. However, the respite created by the fighting between the two kongsis enabled the Dutch to mass for the final assault on Ta-kong which completely destroyed the kongsi in 1854. In spite of a non-aggression pact signed by its fifth President, Liew Tai-irk, with the Dutch in Batavia, Lan-fang's rule lasted only until 1884, thirty years after Ta-kong fell, when, with the death of its tenth and last President, the Dutch brought the kongsi to an end.[2]

BORDER MIGRATION AND BAU KONGSI

On account of the close proximity of Sambas to Upper Sarawak the movement of people across the common border must have taken place from the earliest times. That there were tiny Chinese settlements already in Upper Sarawak, apart from the small trading community living in Kuching when James Brooke first arrived in 1839, is borne out by his own account as related by Robert Payne:

He went a few miles upriver (after a visit to a longhouse) and encountered another race, still more industrious. Here there was a small Chinese settlement of the people newly arrived from Sambas over the border and thirty Chinese men and five Sambas (native) women. They were mining antimony; they had found diamonds and hoped to find tin; they had already planted many acres of rice, betelnut, Indian corn and sweet potatoes. The settlement had been in existence for only four or five months, but already it was flourishing.[3]

But it was the large group of San-Tiou-Kow refugees led by Liew Shan-pang (劉善邦), numbering about 3,000, who gave the border migrations a strong impetus in the nineteenth century. This group soon settled down with their countrymen who had earlier crossed the border in the Bau area of Upper Sarawak, and begun to revive the kongsi system. The majority of these immigrants were absorbed into the kongsi, but there were others who were prepared to take up gold prospecting or agricultural pursuits on their own. And so, while the large Bau kongsi prospered, small units set up by independent miners sprang up, as in the old days in West Borneo.[4] The discovery of antimony in Upper Sarawak in 1823 and the mining of this mineral (1826) on the orders of the Brunei Sultan had served further to increase the mobility of Chinese labour from Sambas to Sarawak.

After the defeat of Ta-kong in 1854 the remnants of this once powerful kongsi also fled across the border to take refuge in Upper Sarawak. The new arrivals, cast in the reverse role of the vanquished seeking sanctuary with their erstwhile rivals and enemies, had little choice in their course of action. They could either throw themselves on the mercy of their hosts, appealing to their magnanimity and sense of fair play to allow them to stay near-by till they could re-establish themselves, or they could, if they were still strong enough, try to take over control of the Bau kongsi which the San-Tiou-Kow group had already set up. Unfortunately history tells us little about what actually happened or what internal struggles for leadership occurred between the two factions. There is an oblique reference to Liew Shan-pang as being the pioneer who opened up the Bau area for settlement and whose memory is still revered. This seems to indicate that it was San-Tiou-Kow and not Ta-kong that won the struggle.

1. Tom Harrisson and Stanley J. O'Connor, 'Gold in West Borneo', *Sarawak Museum Journal*, Vol. XVII, Nos. 34–35, July–December 1969.

2. De Groot, *author of Het Kongsiwezen van Borneo*, has given a detailed account of the kongsi wars. He describes how after the end of the wars the areas were reduced to poor agricultural districts and the mines abandoned. He asks why the Dutch Government left the Javanese their communal institutions and took away those of the Chinese; why this 'sinophobia', this fear of a population which had never given any reason for fear to the Netherlands Government.

3. Robert Payne, *The White Rajahs of Sarawak* (London, 1960).

4. Lo Hsiang-lin gives a list of twelve such small kongsis and states that the list is not exhaustive.

4
The Chinese Rebellion, 1857

PRE-REBELLION EVENTS AND THE TRIAD SOCIETY

WHEN James Brooke became Rajah of Sarawak in 1841,[1] having wrested power from Rajah Muda Hashim and his brother princes of the royal house of Brunei, there was only a small Chinese settlement in Upper Sarawak, a region immediately adjoining the Sultanate of Sambas (in West Kalimantan) where gold had been mined by Chinese kongsis. The settlers had migrated thither from Sambas and settled at first in Pangkalan Tebang just across the border. Later they moved north to Bau where gold and antimony mines were being developed. Like the majority of their compatriots in West Borneo these immigrants were agriculturists cum gold prospectors. No sooner were they settled in the new land than they began to plant food crops and at the same time were on the look out for deposits of alluvial gold, antimony and, even more precious, diamonds, which they would work by panning and sluicing. When their numbers increased they formed themselves into the traditional kongsi for the protection of their interests against outsiders.

By the early 1850s the Chinese population in Upper Sarawak had increased to about 4,000. Following this increase two events occurred. The Chinese miners in West Borneo had learnt that under James Brooke's rule Sarawak had achieved political stability for the first time in many years and that the English Rajah was tolerant of Chinese who opened up land for cultivation and gold prospecting. Against this were the increasingly repressive measures which the Dutch, as new masters of West Borneo, were imposing on the Chinese gold-mining community—measures which led to the use of force which eventually destroyed the kongsis. Accordingly there followed two great migrations into Sarawak: one in 1850 and another between 1854 and 1855. In 1850 a large group of Chinese miners of the San-Tiou-Kow kongsi (三條溝公司) of Pamangkat, who had been attacked and defeated by the more powerful Ta-kong kongsi for siding with the Dutch, fled to Sarawak. They in turn were followed in 1854 by the remnants of the same Ta-kong group who had meanwhile been vanquished by the Dutch and whose kongsi was destroyed.

Once the internal struggle for leadership between the two factions, the San-Tiou-Kow and the Ta-kong, had been resolved, the Bau miners set about reorganizing themselves into one large kongsi and under its aegis mines were operated at Bau, Bidi, Paku, and Tondong. The Bau kongsi duplicated the organization and administration of the old West Borneo kongsis. It also strove to maintain an autonomous status in its dealings with the Rajah's government. The kongsi soon discovered, however, that although the Rajah allowed it to carry on gold mining and agriculture, which produced much-needed revenue for his government, he was by no means prepared to give it the kind of self-governing status that had characterized the West Borneo kongsis in the past. It is necessary to bear this fact in mind if we are to understand fully the motivation of the rebellion which the Bau kongsi organized against James Brooke and his government in 1857.

The Bau kongsi, with its members composed of people coming from the same clan or district in China and speaking more or less the same dialect, was a close-knit community where everyone knew how to pull his weight. Thus in a very short time the kongsi began to thrive.

The mining of gold and other minerals was the kongsi's main occupation. Second came agriculture. Like its predecessors in Sambas the Bau kongsi encouraged its members to grow food crops and to breed domestic animals to supply their own needs; it also gave assistance to independent agriculturists who planted cash crops such as pepper and gambier in areas close to the kongsi.

The West Borneo kongsis, situated ideally near the west coast towns of Sambas and Pontianak, had since their establishment in the middle of the eighteenth century, enjoyed trade and cultural ties with China and a number of South-East Asian countries. The recognition of their autonomous status by the local sultans, before Dutch domination, had enabled the larger kongsis to set up their own bazaars and warehouses as well as their own customs and excise to handle the large volume of import and export trade with foreign lands. In 1834 Earl, who had visited Ta-kong in its heyday and had much praise for its orderly government spoke of his disappointment when he failed to negotiate an agreement for direct trade between the kongsi and Singapore because of Dutch interference.[2] For many years before Dutch control, the kongsis in Sambas were known to be exporting its gold and other local produce to Indo-China and Thailand in exchange for Thai silk and tobacco.[3]

The Bau kongsi, situated close to several rivers flowing directly into the China Sea, could have thrived on similar trade connections with the outside world, but it was not given any opportunity to develop large-scale trading activities because Rajah Brooke never intended to let the kongsi grow to unmanageable proportions. The Rajah in fact regarded the Chinese miners who had fled from Sambas, at best, as refugees and, at worst, as criminals fleeing from Dutch justice. They were permitted to stay and form kongsis to work gold and other minerals merely because the fruit of their labour was of great economic benefit to the country. And the Chinese were good subjects to tax because of their passion for tea, tobacco, opium, and arrack, and their propensity for gambling. James Brooke had first-hand knowledge of the kongsi Chinese. During his first visit to Sarawak in 1839 he had occasion to see a small kongsi in operation in the Bau area and was impressed with the efficiency and industry of the miners. He had decided that the mining kongsis could stay, but the Chinese who operated them must obey his laws to the letter, pay regular taxes, and profess complete allegiance to him and his government. In short the kongsi miners had very few rights, since the Rajah imposed a system of control which made it virtually impossible for them to obtain their supplies except through Sarawak shops, or to export their produce save through the local market. The Rajah exercised a strict monopoly over the sale of opium and arrack and over arrangements for the operation of gambling and pawn farms. After the formation of the Borneo Company in 1856 there was even the possibility that their right to mine gold would be taken away from them.[4]

As the continuance of good relations between the kongsi and the government was wholly dependent on the degree of compliance and subservience shown by the miners, the kongsi continued for a long time to keep the Rajah's good-will. They paid regular taxes and offered humble obeisance and co-operation. Secretly, however, a clandestine trade connection was established with their countrymen across the border and through it they were able to obtain most of the commodities under monopoly in Sarawak, including opium, guns, and ammunition.

Reference should now be made to the Triad Society of China and its influence on the Borneo kongsis in general, and the Bau kongsi of the 1850s in particular. The Triad Society, known in Chinese as T'ien Ti Hueh (天地會), came into being in China in the seventeenth century after the fall of the Ming dynasty. It began as an underground resistance movement organized by those loyal to the Ming, after their overthrow, in order to harass the Ch'ing (Manchu) conquerors with the eventual aim of restoring the Ming dynasty. The word Triad was otherwise known as San Ho (三合) or three united, i.e. a triad union of heaven, earth, and man. The Chinese believed that a perfect unity of these three forces would produce peace and harmony.[5] Their motto was 'Obey heaven and work righteousness'. To its banner initially flocked not only warriors but also patriotic scholars and statesmen. The Triad's political character and revolutionary activities were such that they soon incurred the full wrath of the Manchus. This resulted in many of its leaders and members of the Society being caught and executed, whilst those suspected of complicity in the movement were banished or had to flee from China. They went mostly to the South Sea islands on which large numbers of their countrymen had already settled. They came to Singapore, the crossroads of the east-west traffic; they also arrived in the Dutch East Indies, but they chose in particular the gold fields of West Borneo where the Chinese had worked gold and established kongsis. The kongsis, owing to their autonomous position, their system of organization and their charismatic leadership were found to be most suitable for the revival of the Triad. Nearly all the miners in kongsi employ were of Chinese origin and their sympathies were with China and a Chinese cause. They provided a strong power base for the Triad leaders no less than their presence proved welcome to the kongsi heads who were, generally speaking, men of little education and refinement, though they were brave and independent. The Triad leaders' *savoir-faire* was not lost upon such people. It is not inconceivable that soon some of the Triad men became lieutenants or even advisers to the kongsi heads, and that their advice greatly influenced the policies of the kongsis, leading to the course of action which they later took, for example, in conducting armed resistance against foreign aggressors such as the Dutch. However, there is insufficient evidence to show that the Triad Society at any time gained complete control of the kongsis whether in West Borneo or at Bau, although it is possible that some of the kongsi heads of the seventeenth century and after were themselves Triad leaders or sympathizers in China who, upon reaching Borneo, decided to alter or camouflage their role to suit local conditions.

Whether or not the kongsis were under Triad control, it seems certain that the Triad leaders soon changed their methods of conducting the Society's affairs overseas. The leaders realized that their original cause was lost and that hopes of returning to China were dim. The need to survive made it necessary for them to reorganize themselves into an ambivalent organization which offered both benevolence and anarchical aims. The Sarawak Triad was linked up with a huge network of similar organizations to be found in all parts of the Far East. All were finally accountable to the Triad in China which, in spite of suppression by the Manchus, still thrived underground. The secret nature of the Society, coupled with its secret initiation ceremony and other rituals, and the imposition of a cruel death penalty for defectors, enshrouded it in mystery.

Despite its original motto of 'Obey heaven and work righteousness', the Triad overseas turned into an oligarchy with the sole object of promoting its own wealth and power and dominance over fellow Chinese. It organized protection rackets, offered patronage to vice and gambling and engaged in smuggling contraband goods, including arms and opium. With the mining kongsis offering refuge to Triad members and directly or indirectly encouraging, if not actually taking part in its activities, the Triad Society soon grew to be a formidable institution and it often defied lawful authority. If the leadership of the kongsi was ineffectual, or if the kongsi organization had been completely infiltrated, it may be assumed that the Society would exert sufficient influence to control the kongsi's destiny. Even now the Triad's power and influence are undiminished. Its evil tentacles operating under a cloak of respectability, like the Italian Mafia or Cosa Nostra, have spread throughout the major cities of the Far East, Europe, and America. The secrecy of its organization is retained and it goes by the name of Hung (共).[6]

In the early 1850s the Bau Kongsi apparently enjoyed a period of prosperity. Although dissatisfaction was mounting over the Rajah's monopoly of the sale of opium and over the stern measures he adopted to discourage the growth of Triad influence among the mining community, the Chinese in Bau on the whole still preferred the Rajah's rule which had brought them stability—a stability which made their labour rewarding and their ventures prosperous. This view was not, however, shared by them all, as there was a small group of malcontents and staunch members of the Triad whose activities were being severely curtailed by the Rajah's measures. It is recorded that by the end of the 1850s the Rajah had to warn the principal men of the kongsi about their involvement with the Triad Society. This warning went unheeded and the Rajah ordered the arrest and imprisonment of a Triad agent from Singapore who had come to enrol members by persuasion and threats. In 1852 the kongsi tried to prevent a government officer from arresting a member of the kongsi who had committed an offence. Charles Brooke, Tuan Muda and nephew of the Rajah, was dispatched with some Malays and Dayaks to force the Chinese to give up the man. At this show of force the kongsi gave way. As a punishment the Rajah ordered the Chinese to build and equip a fort at Belidah, just below Bau, as an observation post to check on their movements. This fort was put under the charge of Sharif Matusain and a garrison of Malays. Charles Brooke also demanded that one hundred muskets owned by the Chinese should be handed over to the government but the Rajah rescinded the order.

Punitive action such as that just described deepened the miners' feeling of resentment against the Rajah and his government, a resentment further aggravated by the manner in which the monopoly of the supply opium was regulated. After the Opium War and the signing of the Treaty of Nanking in 1842, the sale of opium to the Chinese was no longer under strict control. This habit-forming, debilitating drug then came to be used liberally as a stimulant by all classes of Chinese, from high-ranking mandarins to labourers engaged in heavy labour. James Brooke endeavoured to improve the welfare of all his people, but he was not averse to the import and regular sale of opium to the Chinese to earn state revenue. He also determined how much opium a Chinese community ought to use, and exacted a tax for that amount. In the Bau kongsi the amount of opium bought by the miners was reported as having fallen below the previously determined level. This led him to believe that the kongsi, under Triad control, was smuggling in opium from other sources and selling it to the smokers. The Rajah therefore insisted that the kongsi pay for the full quota of opium irrespective of how much the miners actually purchased. In January 1857, the kongsi was fined £150 for illicitly smuggling opium. The fine was paid, but with increasing resentment against the Brooke government.

The events then occurring in Sarawak were not unconnected with those happening in China. In October 1856, there was trouble once more between the Chinese and the English merchants in Canton. Commissioner Yeh publicly offered a monetary reward of 30 dollars for every English head delivered to him. Soon a rumour began to circulate in *nanyang* that the English in Canton had been massacred. In January 1857 there was an unsuccessful uprising by the Chinese in Singapore. The Bau kongsi heard these reports and also knew that the Rajah was in disgrace in England where he was the subject of a Royal Commission of Enquiry regarding his handling of the suppression of piracy. They concluded that England would not come to his aid.

THE REBELLION, OCCUPATION OF KUCHING, AND DEFEAT

Suffering from what they considered to be unduly harsh and unfair treatment at the hands of the Rajah, the kongsi Chinese, incited by the Triad elements in their midst, had been for some time contemplating the use of force to overthrow the Rajah's government. For this purpose they secretly collected arms and weapons. Their plan was to stage a *coup d'état* and kill the Rajah and his European colleagues. Their object was more to ensure that the kongsi's old way of life could continue rather than to take over the government and set up their own administration.

Thinking the time was now opportune for action, the Bau kongsi mobilized a force of 600 able-bodied men and on 18 February 1857, one month after the payment of the £150 fine, they made their way from Tondong to Kuching by boat. They arrived shortly after midnight and, dividing themselves into two parties, they began to attack the Rajah's house on the left bank of the Sarawak River and simultaneously Kuching town on its right bank, where government offices and commercial buildings were situated. Never believing that the Chinese had the temerity or the strength to launch an attack on Kuching (although he had been warned of the miners' intentions) and being thoroughly unprepared, James Brooke had to flee for his life. He took temporary refuge in the house of a Malay official after swimming across a creek under the bow of a boat. A few Europeans, including two children, were killed by the rebels and several others were wounded. The Rajah's house and houses occupied by his officers were razed to the ground. The other party of Chinese attacking Kuching town had no difficulty in occupying the court-house and other government buildings, the only resistance they met with was that put up by the Rajah's two manned stockades. The Chinese did not, however, destroy the court-house, nor did they attack the neighbouring Malay kampungs or the Chinese shophouses in the bazaar, although most of the latter were in sympathy with the Rajah's administration. The remaining Europeans whose houses were not burnt by the rebels gathered, some with their families, at the house of the Anglican Bishop, Francis McDougall, who was well-known and respected as a church leader as well as a surgeon. By morning the rebels were in full possession of Kuching town. At first light the next day a delegation of seven Chinese came to the Bishop's house to seek the latter's help for their wounded. They assured the Bishop that their quarrel was only with the Rajah and his men and not with the Europeans in general.

Later that morning the Chinese leaders sent for Ludvig Helms, Manager of the Borneo Company who traded with the Bau kongsi, an English merchant called Rupell, Bishop McDougall, and the Datu Bandar, the Malay chief, to appear before them in the court-house. After demanding that all present swear an oath of allegiance to the kongsi under threat of instant death, their leader[7] made it clear that the kongsi had no intention of running the government itself. They wished to appoint Helms and Rupell to rule the foreign section of the town while the Datu Bandar would rule the Malays in Kuching, but the kongsi would be the supreme ruler. Those present seized the opportunity to remind the Chinese that the Rajah was still alive and that his nephew, the Tuan Muda, who had the support of cohorts of Ibans was only temporarily away in Skrang and would return to exact retribution. Somewhat apprehensive, the Chinese leaders decided to write a letter to Charles Brooke to the effect that 'river water does not trespass on well water', that they would not interfere with him so long as he did not interfere with them and confined himself to the districts he governed.

The next day the Chinese withdrew to Bau from Kuching taking with them the loot they had seized from the European houses and government buildings. But the news that the Malays were rallying round the Rajah to offer active resistance soon brought them back from Bau with large reinforcements. They stayed on in Kuching town in spite of many efforts made by the Rajah and his Malay allies to dislodge them. The Chinese retaliated by burning down Malay houses on both sides of the river. The rebels remained entrenched till Charles Brooke arrived from Skrang with his Iban warriors. There then began a two-pronged attack by Ibans led by Charles Brooke and Malays loyal to the Rajah. The attack was directed by James Brooke himself from the Borneo Company steamer *James Brooke* (which had made a timely arrival from Singapore), and dominated by the firing of the ship's guns. The kongsi Chinese were routed and retreated in great disorder upriver to Bau where they were relentlessly pursued by the

Rajah's men and driven across the border to Sambas. Thousands were killed. The Sambas Chinese, irked by their unwelcome arrival and the disaster they had brought on everyone fell on the remnants and killed many more. The Dutch government of West Borneo recovered some of the loot taken by the rebels from Sarawak and sent it back to the Sarawak government.

This is more or less the story of the Chinese rebellion according to recorded history. Western writers reviewing the events from the perspective of the colonial administration were apt to describe the kongsi Chinese who took part in the rebellion as criminals who had fled from Dutch justice or as members of the Triad Society whose resentment against the Rajah was caused by the fact that he had severely punished them for their extortionist and other anti-social activities. Such over-simplified and one-sided opinions have for many years clouded judgements on a very important period of Chinese history in Sarawak. They tended to paint a picture of the early Chinese settlers in Sarawak as the dregs of Chinese society who, when welcomed into a foreign land, soon plotted and connived with their fellow countrymen to bite the hands that fed them. In fact for many years little else was considered worth knowing about the kongsi Chinese. Fortunately with improved scholarship on the subject in recent years new facts have been brought to light which enable a more balanced verdict to be formed without prejudice.

The Bau kongsi Chinese cannot be entirely exonerated from the blame of starting a rebellion which had caused much loss of life and property, and which certainly set back good Sino-European relations in Sarawak, not to mention the country's economic progress, for many years. But a fair analysis of the circumstances and events of that time does not absolve the Rajah and his government from responsibility either. The Chinese miners who came from West Borneo to Bau were once proud members of self-governing communities. They belonged to a race with an ancient culture and heritage and in Borneo they had learnt how to govern themselves.

True, they were conscious of their refugee status and aware of their debt to the Rajah's government, but they had also expected just treatment at the hands of a reputedly benevolent English ruler. Instead they found themselves tolerated by a government that viewed them with suspicion and treated them with great severity for every deviation from the white man's laws. James Brooke, on the other hand, was a product of the Victorian age, which saw the height of Britain's achievements and prestige. He was essentially a colonialist and, like all other European colonialists, had his own set of values. These values stressed the superiority of the white man and his culture; all other cultures, including Chinese, were inferior. James Brooke, being more of an idealist than most, considered it his duty to replace this inferior Chinese culture with 'proper' culture for men.[8] Throughout his relationship with the Chinese neither he nor his officers made any effort to try to understand them or their attitude to life. Whenever they failed to toe the official line they had to be humbled and firmly suppressed. Had there been any attempt to study their needs and to provide correct answers to their problems, based on human dignity and mutual dependence and respect, a sensible approach would have been found and the rebellion could have been averted.

1. In 1841 Sarawak as a state consisted of land lying roughly between Tanjung Datu and the Samarahan River and inland to the border with Sambas. Known as Sarawak Proper, it approximates to the area of the present First Division.

2. G. W. Earl, *The Eastern Seas*.

3. This information was obtained from the oral reminiscences of an elderly Chinese ex-resident of Sambas whose forebears were traders in Sambas towards the close of the kongsi rule.

4. In 1856 James Brooke approved the formation of the Borneo Company and gave it the exclusive right to work all minerals, except gold, provided a fixed annual rent was paid to the government for each mineral worked. Gold, until then, had been mined by the Chinese. Some writers surmise the one of the causes of the Bau Chinese kongsi's

rebellion in 1857 was the miners' fear that their right to mine gold would also be taken away from them and given to the Company to monopolize.

5. Baring-Gould and Bampfylde, *A History of Sarawak under its Two White Rajahs, 1839–1908*, pp. 186–7.

6. See Harry Arvay's novel, based on fact, *Triad 21* (New English Library/Times Mirror, 1977).

7. It is a pity that there is no record anywhere of who or what he was.

8. J. R. Hipkins, 'History of the Chinese in Borneo', *Sarawak Museum Journal*, Vol. XIX, Nos. 38–39, July–December, 1971, p. 128.

5
Post-Rebellion Chinese Pioneers

EARLY PIONEERS

ONE direct result of the Chinese rebellion was that for some time there were practically no Chinese miners left in the Bau area after the kongsi's defeat. The previously flourishing gold mines and pepper plantations which had provided the Rajah's government with most of its revenue lay deserted; the opium, arrack,[1] and gambling farms which had yielded handsome taxes were silent. The very few Chinese merchants and residents of Kuching town (people who had come from China through Singapore or one of the islands of the Malay archipelago and who shared little or no dialect affinity or clan relationship with the West Borneo Chinese) had supported the Rajah during the rebellion and had survived the crisis, but their businesses were ruined because they, like everyone else in Sarawak, had depended a good deal on the gold mines for their own prosperity.

The memory of the 1857 rebellion would always rankle in the Rajah's mind. To the end of his life he would regard all Chinese with great caution and misgiving, trusting only those he had come to know well. The rebellion had taught him and his administration an important lesson: that a country could not thrive on the authority and prestige of its leadership alone. This rebellion had also exhausted his personal resources and left his treasury with empty coffers. The destruction of the Bau kongsi meant that his main source of revenue was cut off. Realizing the seriousness of his situation and appreciating that only Chinese industry and enterprise could get the country back on its feet, James Brooke began to see the unwisdom of his past policies, and little by little he adopted a more conciliatory attitude towards the Chinese. This change of attitude was later followed by his European officers and colleagues, notably his nephew and successor, Charles Johnson Brooke, the Tuan Muda. It was reflected by the Rajah encouraging Chinese merchants to resume the export of Sarawak produce to Singapore and to intensify their efforts on large-scale cultivation of pepper and gambier, as well as the processing and refining of raw sago.

As time passed more and more of the kongsi Chinese who had taken refuge in Sambas after the rebellion drifted back to Bau, bringing others with them, and they rebuilt their old homes.[2] Some time after the rebellion the Rajah gave permission to a group of loyal Hakka Chinese under the leadership of Liew Syn Ted (劉新德), who had previously settled along the Sadong River east of Kuching, to move into the mining areas to re-establish the gold workings.[3] The newly formed Borneo Company, which was to take over and amalgamate all the mines in 1898, meanwhile lent equipment to individual mining groups and provided a stamp mill for crushing coarse gold ore. To pave the way for Chinese agriculturists to settle permanently James Brooke drew up the first land law in 1863 which became the basis of later land legislation. This law conferred on the Chinese the right to obtain leases of State land in return for the payment of a fee simple.

The increasingly favourable atmosphere created for Chinese settlement in Sarawak soon attracted more people to join the small group of early pioneers living in and around Kuching, some of whom had established themselves before the rebellion. Of this early group little is known or recorded with the exception of four men, three of whom are credited with being the founders of their own communities in Sarawak.

They are Lau Chek (劉直), Ong Ewe Hai (王友海), Chan Kho (田考), and Law Kian Huat (劉建發). All except Lau Chek were traders who prospered and later became prominent merchants and pillars of the Chinese society. They were trusted by the Rajah and in turn developed into an influential local plutocracy, ready to mobilize the resources of the business community in support of his regime. They formed a triumvirate to whom the Rajah looked for help in controlling the Chinese and whose advice was sought in all matters pertaining to Chinese culture and custom.

Lau Chek's name does not appear in Chinese records consulted for this work. According to European sources he was a Cantonese who had arrived in Sarawak a decade or so before James Brooke first set foot on its soil. Lau Chek came by junk with a few friends, sailing direct from China to Simanggang (in the present Second Division) about 1830, and thence they made their way to Satok, Kuching, to take up land for cultivating vegetables and breeding livestock. He later became the Rajah's steward and fought on the Rajah's side with his followers during the rebellion. He is believed to have been the person alluded to by Runciman,[4] an official historian of the colonial period who, in defence of the first Rajah not being prejudiced against the Chinese, cited as proof that his steward was Chinese.

Ong Ewe Hai was born in Singapore. His family had come from T'ung-ann district in Fukien province. Having lost his father as a boy, Ong Ewe Hai had to assume the role of family provider at the age of sixteen. This he did by becoming a petty trader. News of the lucrative barter trade with the natives of Sarawak soon sent him to Kuching in 1846 with an older partner, Lim Eng Moh. Notwithstanding the tedious sea journey which at that time took seven to ten days between Singapore and Sarawak, and the primitive living conditions he had to put up with on arrival, he immediately set to work and soon built up a partnership business under the name of Ewe Hai, Moh & Co. He travelled often between Kuching and Singapore, returning on each trip with the merchandise and goods needed in Sarawak. His straightforward nature and honest dealings soon earned him a good name in the Singapore trading community. In 1856, ten years after he had founded the Sarawak firm, he launched a similar firm in Singapore and called it Kay Cheang, Ewe Hai & Co. After 1872 the firm's name was changed to Ong Ewe Hai & Co., and the same name was retained for his firm in Sarawak. Ong Ewe Hai retired to Singapore in his old age leaving the Sarawak business in the capable hands of his Sarawak-born son, Ong Tiang Swee, who in due course was to outshine his father both as an entrepreneur and as the foremost leader of the Chinese community. Ong Ewe Hai died in 1889.

Chan Kho is recognized as the founder of the Chao-ann community in Sarawak. He was a native of Chao-ann district, Fukien province. Hailing from a very poor branch of the Chan (T'ien) clan, Chan Kho, like many a young man of his time, had only one ambition—to improve his family fortune by joining the increasing number of emigrants venturing into the South Seas. This he did at the age of eighteen by signing himself on as a crew member in a small sailing boat carrying salt from a Fukien port. He arrived in Kuching in 1846 and went to Bau to work as a labourer for a clansman who spoke the Hakka dialect. He found traces of gold in the garden where he worked and turned to prospecting. He did sufficiently well to branch out on his own as a rural shopkeeper, selling tobacco and sundry goods. He prospered and moved to Kuching to extend his business activities which had meanwhile developed from dealing in native produce to buying and selling real estate. His Midas touch made him immensely wealthy. He applied to the Rajah for permission to bring in more Chao-anns from China to settle in Sarawak. He died in 1904. His son Chan Kay Soon, born in Sarawak, took over his business and became a well-known and trusted Chinese community leader in his own time.

Law Kian Huat, the Teochew pioneer, arrived from Swatow through Singapore about 1852 with a group of fellow villagers. They engaged in the cultivation of gambier and pepper along

Penrissen Road, Kuching, and at Batu Kawa and Bako in the coastal area. Law Kian Huat then entered into business partnership with a fellow clansman, Sim Ah Nio, and established in 1854 the import and export firm of Ghee Soon & Co. Under his capable management all his ventures prospered. Soon Law Kian Huat was able to obtain James Brooke's approval to bring in more Teochew agriculturists from China to extend his gambier and pepper plantations. Ghee Soon & Co., with the Rajah's encouragement, was also engaged in refining raw sago for export. This, for many years, remained a lucrative business. With success came more business opportunities. For nearly twenty years Ghee Soon & Co. successfully retained the tenders for gambling, arrack, and opium farms which were held under government monopoly. Law Kian Huat's social position and his business enterprises rivalled those of the Hokkien leader, Ong Ewe Hai. It was known that the Rajah from time to time had taken loans from Ghee Soon & Co. when the State finances ran into unexpected difficulties. Law Kian Huat is therefore credited with encouraging the immigration of Teochews into Sarawak and laying the foundation of their community. He died in 1885.

The biographies of these three pioneers are given in some detail because of the important place they hold in the history of Sarawak's Chinese community after the rebellion. Their active life spans covered the second half of the nineteenth century. They were leaders of the first epoch which ended with the death of James Brooke in 1868. The second epoch began and ended with Charles Brooke's rule, 1868–1917. It saw the emergence of a number of new leaders, two of whom were the sons of Ong Ewe Hai and Chan Kho. The number of such leaders increased at the turn of the century when the second Rajah's land settlement policy attracted large influxes of new immigrants from China to take up land concessions. For easy reference a list of early Chinese community leaders who held the centre of the stage between 1841 and 1910 is appended (see pp. 45–8). The list is by no means exhaustive.

The Chinese leaders mentioned in this list belonged to the

EARLY CHINESE LEADERSHIP IN SARAWAK, 1841–1910

Name	Origin and Other Particulars	Occupation or Economic Activities	Social Activities or Achievements
Ong Ewe Hai (1818–89) 王友海	T'ung-ann District, Fukien. Born in Singapore but came to settle and trade in Kuching from 1846	Barter trade with Sarawak natives. Activities extended to import and export business, etc. Established Ewe Hai & Co. both in Sarawak and Singapore.	Hokkien Community leader; first Rajah's trusted adviser and appointed head of Sarawak Chinese Community.
Chan Kho (1828–1904) 田考	Chao-ann District, Fukien Province. Arrived in Sarawak at age of 18.	Labouring and gold-prospecting. Activities later extended to business and real estate.	Head of Chao-ann Community; one of first Rajah's trusted advisers on Chinese affairs.
Law Kian Huat (1835–85) 劉建發	Chaochow, Kwangtung Province; came to Sarawak as a young man.	Cultivation of pepper and gambier; established Ghee Soon & Co.; running opium, arrack & gambling farms on government contract.	Teochew Community leader and one of first Rajah's trusted advisers; organizer for erection of Heavenly King Temple (for Teochews) and its main donor.
Yeo Ban Hock (Guan Cho) (1858–1925) 楊萬福(元藻)	Chang-t'ai District, Fukien Province. Arrived in Sarawak in 1877.	Import and export business; building construction; running opium, arrack & gambling farms on government contract.	Contractor for Hokkien Free School building and one of its donors; main donor for erection of Lim Hua Shan Temple; constructed the Ban Hock Wharf.

Name	Origin and Other Particulars	Occupation or Economic Activities	Social Activities or Achievements
Ong Tiang Swee (1864–1950) 王長水	Born in Sarawak, son of Ong Ewe Hai. Educated in English.	Took over from father and developed family business; later branched out into new fields of shipping and banking. Manager of Ong Ewe Hai & Co. and a director of Sarawak Steamship Co.	Hokkien Community leader; chief founder of Hokkien Free School; held in high esteem by second and third Rajahs; served for many years as President of Chinese Court of Justice and made Kapitan China of Sarawak. Made life member of Supreme Council by third Rajah and invited to attend Council Negri meetings pre-war.
Chan Kay Soon (1865–1910) 田祈順	Born in Sarawak, son of Chan Kho. Educated in Chinese and English.	Succeeded to father's business. Manager of Chop Chin Ann.	A founder of Hokkien Free School. Co-sponsor of several temples and places of worship.
Tan Boh Seng (Ah Boh) (1870–1924) 陳戌辰 (亞戌)	Chaochow, Kwangtung Province; came to Singapore in his teens; migrated to Kuching at age of 19.	Engaged in pepper and gambier cultivation; operated Semengok quarry, 7th Mile, Penrissen Road, for many years.	Teochew Community leader. Began as bookkeeper to Lee Soon Kheng's pepper and gambier plantation at Semengok (Sam Hup Hin Kang), 7th Mile, Penrissen Road. In 1899 was made its Kangchew by

Name	Origin and Other Particulars	Occupation or Economic Activities	Social Activities or Achievements
			Rajah Charles Brooke. Supporter of R. C. Mission and its Chinese medium school at Semengok.
Lee Cheng Tien (1875–1965) 李振殿	Hai-cheng District, Fukien Province. Came to Sarawak at age of 22. Migrated to Singapore in 1912.	Established business in Kuching and Sibu, dealing in native produce.	Hokkien Community leader. Supporter of the revolution started by Dr Sun Yat Sen to overthrow the Manchus. More active subsequent to his migration to Singapore.
Song Kheng Hai (1876–1945) 宋慶海	Nan-ann District, Fukien Province. Followed his father to Sarawak at an early age.	Import and export business and building construction. Failed in business during depression years of 1930s.	Hokkien Community leader. Appointed magistrate in the Chinese Court of Justice.
Wong Nai Siong (1849–1924) 黃乃裳	Min-tsing District, Fukien Province. Passed Ching imperial exams. and became jeu-ren (舉人) scholar and visionary; supporter of Dr Sun Yat Sen's	Signed agreement with Rajah Charles Brooke in 1900 and led more than 1,000 Foochows to settle in Sibu. Returned to	Foochow pioneer, leader and Kangchew. Responsible for erecting a number of churches (Methodist) and two schools for the settlers.

Name	Origin and Other Particulars	Occupation or Economic Activities	Social Activities or Achievements
	revolution to overthrow the Manchus.	China in 1906.	
Tang Kung Suk (1855–1925) 鄧恭淑	San-sui District, Kwangtung Province. Also passed the Ching imperial exams. and became a *jeu-ren* (district level scholar). Supporter of Dr Sun Yat Sen's revolution.	In 1902 led followers (Cantonese) to take up land concessions in Rejang basin above Sibu. Subsequently returned to China.	Became *Kangchew* of the settlers.
Teo Chong Loh (1877–1958) 張宗羅	Hai-cheng District, Fukien Province. Arrived in Sibu 1892 via Singapore.	Dealer in agricultural and native produce; established banking business	Hokkien Community leader. Appointed Kapitan China in Sibu. Established Chung Hua Primary School in Sibu.

second epoch. An analysis of the leadership structure of the early Sarawak Chinese and its effect on the subsequent development of the Chinese community is given in another chapter.

EXTENSION OF SARAWAK'S TERRITORY

Large-scale Chinese immigration into Sarawak did not begin until after Charles Brooke became Rajah in 1868. During his lifetime James Brooke's government had remained weak in the remote areas which thus required frequent military action to counteract local lawlessness; besides his fear and mistrust

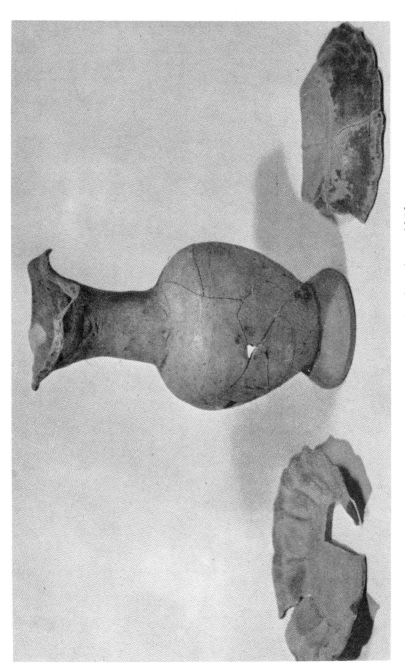

1. Early T'ang Ewer Excavated at Santubong, 1956

2. Chinese Goldminers, Bau

3. Sarawak River and Kuching Town, 1839

4. Chinese Shops along Main Bazaar, 1880

5. Ong Ewe Hai

6. Law Kian Huat

7. Wong Nai Siong, sketch from an old photograph

8. Ong Tiang Swee

of the Chinese after the 1857 rebellion persisted for a long time. Furthermore the country under his rule was at first limited in extent. It comprised only Sarawak Proper, which is roughly the land lying between Tanjung Datu and the Samarahan River and inland to the border with Sambas. It was not until 1853 that this frontier was extended to include land between the Samarahan and the Saribas/Rejang watershed, ceded to him by the Sultan of Brunei for suppressing the marauding inland native tribes who often attacked the rich sago lands near the coast. This area came to be known as the Second Division. In 1861, a few years before the end of the Rajah's life, more land was ceded in the Rejang, Oya, Mukah, Tatau, and Bintulu River basins. This land had been under the ineffectual control of the Brunei Sultan's representatives who had sought the Rajah's help to quell local revolts led by rebel chieftains. It was ceded to the Rajah in return for the payment of an annual grant of $4,500 to the Sultan. The three areas of Rejang, Mukah, and Oya later comprised the Third Division.

Charles Brooke continued to extend the boundaries of Sarawak. In 1882 he took over the Baram, land that was inhabited mainly by Kayans who had revolted against Brunei rule. This area, together with Bintulu and Tatau, became known as the Fourth Division. In 1885 Trusan was ceded to Sarawak at the Sultan's request as he was no longer able to suppress local rebellions. The annual grant paid for this additional territory was $4,500 per annum. Limbang was annexed in 1890. Finally in 1905 the Lawas River basin was transferred to Sarawak from the British North Borneo Company. The three areas of Limbang, Lawas, and Trusan therefore became the Fifth Division. Thus Sarawak grew to its present size.[5]

1. Arrack is a locally distilled whisky having a high percentage of alcohol.

2. Although formal migrations began to peter out after the 1860s,

border crossings by individual mining and agricultural groups between Sambas and Bau or Lundu, and vice versa, continued well into the late 1870s. The issue of border passes after 1872 stopped large-scale border migrations.

3. Liew Syn Ted remained on good terms with the Rajah's government. He served for many years as magistrate in Upper Sarawak under the rule of Charles Brooke (*Sarawak Gazette*, July 1913).

4. Steven Runciman, *The White Rajahs* (Cambridge University Press, 1960).

5. After the formation of Malaysia the State of Sarawak was divided into more Divisions for convenience of administration and development. The Third Division, with the largest land area, was divided into three separate Divisions: 3rd (chief town Sibu), 6th (chief town Sarikei), and 7th (chief town Kapit).

6

Chinese Immigration and Development of Agriculture, 1863—1941

CHINESE IMMIGRANTS: RECRUITED, FREE, AND SPONSORED GROUPS

WITH such vast territories which needed to be developed coming under his rule Charles Brooke soon intensified his efforts to bring in more Chinese immigrants. Like his uncle he had certain prejudices against the Chinese, but unlike James Brooke Charles was a far better administrator. He was practical, resolute, and fearless. He had always had great admiration for Chinese industry and business acumen. His practical mind saw their potential very soon after his arrival in Sarawak in 1852. When visiting Lundu as a young officer he had observed the hundreds of acres of Chinese gardens planted with food and cash crops and remarked that the Chinese had a wonderful knack of making the most of a bit of ground. In 1866, five years after the annexation of the Rejang basin he wrote that if there was to be an influx of Chinese agriculturists he thought the Rejang would be the most suitable place for them to settle. He envisioned the area being connected by road links to other places and served by large vessels sailing up the Rejang.[1] The 1857 rebellion did not alter Charles' opinion of the Chinese in the way that it upset James Brooke. As he was responsible for crushing the rebellion, he found himself able

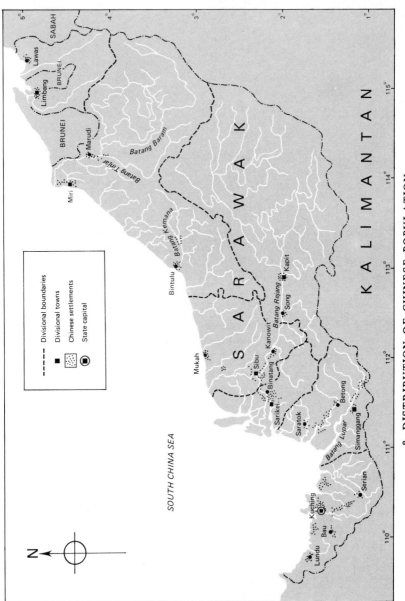

3. DISTRIBUTION OF CHINESE POPULATION

to deal with the Chinese from a position of strength, confident of his authority and ability to keep them in check. The Chinese, too, saw in this white man a strong and decisive ruler who kept a firm hand over the turbulent tribes and at the same time was capable and resourceful enough to turn Sarawak into a stable and prosperous state. Thus during his rule both the more cultured merchants and other urban dwellers and the rough miners and unlettered rural settlers showed him due deference and offered him their sincere co-operation. As his rule became stronger this co-operation covered not only finance and agriculture but was extended to Chinese immigration.

With the organization of the notorious coolie (labour) trade after China's defeat and the signing of the Peking Treaty in 1860, Britain began increasingly to recruit large numbers of Chinese labourers for service in its colonies and other outposts of its wide-spread empire. This produced the system of labour brokers who operated both in the treaty ports and outside China. They undertook to recruit indentured or contract labour for the tin mines, and later rubber plantations of Java and Malaya, the sugar plantations of Cuba and the West Indies, and the gold mines and railroads of California. The brokers grew rich on the trade; so did the owners who recruited the labourers. That these labourers were often treated inhumanly and had to put up with their contracts being 'renewed' indefinitely till old age or infirmity made it impossible for them to gain their liberty did not apparently worry the owners or the brokers. From the 1860s until the First World War the contract labour system was in full operation. The hub of the labour market for South-East Asia was Singapore which being geographically close to Kuching was already commercially linked with both Chinese and European firms in Sarawak. Not surprisingly, therefore, Singapore was for many years an important source of Chinese labour for the Sarawak market.

At this time when contract Chinese labour came to Sarawak the Rajah's government was directly involved. Charles Brooke set up an agency in Singapore (A. L. Johnson & Co.

and later Paterson, Simons & Co.) to handle the details of procuring labourers. This agency also procured the Indian labourers the Rajah needed to work on government estates and to build roads, but their numbers were limited. Through the Singapore agency and another that Charles Brooke established in Labuan in the 1880s, he obtained a number of Chinese labourers for the government-operated coal mines at Sadong and Brooketon, and the experimental tobacco and tea plantations at Matang. Thus the recruited contract labourers became the forerunners of the massive influx of Chinese immigrants who entered Sarawak in the post-rebellion period, and who laid the foundation of agriculture as a rural industry rather than as a subsidiary to mining.

The system of recruiting labourers through Singapore was unsatisfactory for Sarawak. The recruits who came as emigrants from China or from other parts of South-East Asia were more often than not the riff-raff of society—criminals, debtors, the insane, or the physically unfit. Charles Brooke had no control over their selection. It was not until after 1877 that a Chinese Protectorate was set up by the Straits Settlement Government with the object of improving the coolie trade. The physical checks carried out by the Protectorate on the labourers to determine their fitness to work were, however, very perfunctory; and the unhealthy conditions in the depots where the labourers were held rendered many useless for work afterwards. Compared with the contract labourers, the Rajah could see how much stronger was the physique of the free labourers brought over by Chinese merchants and planters, or at their request, to take up work in their plantations.

After 1890 improvements were introduced by Singapore as a result of Sarawak's protests, and the Rajah responded by promulgating a new law which provided, among other things, a depot in Kuching to house and care for the new arrivals in clean and hygienic surroundings, until their labour contracts were properly drawn up and witnessed by a Brooke official and their assignments made. The Rajah also provided assisted passages in one of the government's steamers to enable the recruited labourers to travel without charge from Singapore to Sarawak. The supply was, nevertheless, uncertain and inadequate, and by 1914 the Singapore source had dwindled to a trickle.[2]

Dissatisfied with the quality of the labour recruits from Singapore the Rajah consulted the Chinese merchants in Kuching to make plans for the direct recruitment of labourers from China. The high cost involved at first made the plan impractical. After the 1870s Sarawak's economy began to pick up and in the following decades the country's increasing prosperity caused an acute labour shortage. This once more focused attention on the China source of supply. The cost of obtaining labour from China had, if anything, increased yet further in the mean time, but it was compensated by the better physical condition of the direct arrivals. Charles Brooke was so impressed that from then on he decided to use the Chinese merchants as his recruiting agents.

Apart from Chinese labourers recruited through agencies as already described, large numbers of free immigrants entered Sarawak, that is those who came of their own accord, either in response to offers made for labourers or to join relatives and friends previously settled in Sarawak. Most of the free immigrants were hired by Chinese and, in some cases, European business interests, for agricultural work and in the mining industry. There were several sources for this category of immigrants, but Singapore remained the most important transit port for Sarawak. The vast majority arrived direct from China, but there were others who had taken service in the Dutch East Indies and the Straits Settlements. At a later date the free immigrants tended more to belong to the non-labouring classes: traders who thought business prospects in Sarawak promising, planters lured by generous Brooke land offers, craftsmen, artisans, and intellectuals who came, one and all, to offer their skills and knowledge to a growing country. The free immigrants were usually sponsored by prominent Chinese leaders or merchants who stood well with the government and who might have accepted commissions from planters and others to recruit labourers for work in Sarawak, or who had obtained specific approval from the Rajah to bring over groups from their own clans or districts to provide the necessary labour in their agricultural or industrial ventures. Some of these leaders appointed agents or brokers to collect and accompany the new recruits (generally called *sinkhehs* 新客) on their outward journey from China; others preferred to become their own agents. They returned to China from time to time for this purpose and at the same time to visit the families they had probably left behind. The Teochew leader, Law Kian Huat, is recorded as having made two trips to Swatow in the 1880s to recruit labourers for Sarawak.

The following graphic contemporary account given by Chater of the arrival of free immigrants direct from China, and of the scramble of agents who went on board the junk to sign up the exhausted voyagers, makes interesting reading:

The junks always came during the time of the northeast monsoon (*landas*) when the wind was in their favour. . . . The decks were always crowded with coolies especially after the great flood of the Yellow River in 1889 when disaster swept over a large part of China. A few who had been lucky enough to make money in Sarawak had returned to their native land and rumours soon spread, 'Sarawak, land of gold'. The life of a coolie in China at that time was a constant struggle to earn enough to eat and so it is easy to understand why they were ready to undertake the hardships of a journey by a small junk to Sarawak.

The junks tossed about like corks in the rough sea and the passengers were packed so closely that they could hardly move. They were sea sick and unable to eat a ration which, in any case, only consisted of one bowl of rice a day and one teaspoonful of water three times a day. . . .

It was never known for certain how long a journey would take since, being entirely dependent on sails, it mostly depended on the sea and wind, but normally it took a month. . . . The men more dead than alive, were engaged even before the junk bringing them in had dropped anchor. Look outs were posted at the mouth of the Sarawak River and, as soon as the junks were sighted, a mad scramble started to board them as quickly as possible and press half a year's advance salary of $30 into each man's hand, thus buying him almost body and soul at the rate of eighteen cents a day. Most of it went to the broker (who came with

them). These men were much sought after as physically they were
much stronger than those who arrived from Singapore. . . .[3]

The account, though naïve in some respects, does highlight
the hardships suffered by the free immigrants during their sea
voyage to Sarawak from China by junk and the impecunious
state of each immigrant. Indeed the free immigrant was financially little better off than the indentured labourer. As
poverty was one of the reasons for an immigrant to leave
home and risk his life overseas, few if any could pay their
passage which was usually paid for them in advance by the bro-
ker, to be recovered after their arrival in Sarawak and assign-
ment to an employer. Immigrants who had a relative or kins-
man to sponsor them were luckier, but in any case all immigrants would be dependent on their employers and be beholden
to them financially and socially. Most employers, and generally the sponsors, were people of the same clan or district
and shared a common dialect with the immigrants. Consequently an immigrant normally found himself beginning his
new life in Sarawak either as an apprentice in the employer's
trade or occupation, if they both lived in the town, or as a
labourer if the employer had agricultural holdings in the
country. This natural division by occupation of the free immigrant in relation to that of his employer or sponsor, coupled with traditional clan connection and dialect grouping,
largely determined his occupational identification and geographical distribution in Sarawak. Further details will be included later.

Mention was made earlier of James Brooke's land law of
1863 which became the framework of the Brooke land policy.
With amendments made by Charles Brooke this law was responsible for attracting Chinese immigrants to Sarawak and
Chinese capital to flow in from near-by Singapore, thus laying the foundation for large-scale agricultural development.
Between 1875 and 1888 Singapore and Sarawak Chinese merchants were associated in at least three major government-
sponsored companies established for the cultivation of gam-

bier and pepper crops in several areas of Sarawak, notably in Lundu in the First Division.[4] The major provisions of the 1863 law were that the State held claim to all land unless it was disposed of in public sale or granted to any one by the Rajah; that land would be leased for 999 years, but could be bought upon payment of a fee simple of $1.00 for each acre after being leased for three years; that the government reserved the right to re-enter any land whether upon lease or bought by payment if not being properly utilized; that squatters had no right to their land; and that the State owned all mineral rights.[5] Charles Brooke reaffirmed this law in 1871 but added several amendments which gave added compensation rights to occupants of land and claimed certain areas for public purposes. At the same time he made attractive offers to encourage large-scale Chinese settlers. These offers became well-known throughout the East Indies by the 1880s. He also ensured that the customary land rights of the Malays and especially of the Dayaks, who claimed large tracts customarily for their shifting cultivation, were preserved and respected. This he did by issuing, during his rule, a series of proclamations governing land matters (e.g. specifying the locality and size of settlement lots and laying down conditions for their occupation, including the offer of free sea passages from Singapore to the settlers and financiers). These were modified from time to time. In the main he was able to achieve his primary purpose of attracting Chinese settlers to open up large areas of land for agriculture and to confine their development schemes to specified localities. By judicious warnings and advice to the Dayaks and Malays the Rajah forestalled their tendency to sell land to all takers, thus preventing foreign, particularly European, speculators and exploiters from gaining control of their land, as had happened in North Borneo and parts of Malaya.[6] It is said that the Rajah feared Chinese encroachment less than the possible appearance in Sarawak of a European planter class. This fear of European speculators characterized the Brooke government from 1841 to 1945, but it was a boon to Chinese settlers who thus faced little competition in the agricultural field and also came to occupy the important place they now hold in the country's economy.

AGRICULTURAL SETTLEMENTS IN FIRST, THIRD, AND OTHER DIVISIONS

Charles Brooke's land offers became the cornerstone of state policy for Chinese immigration and settlement; and they drew large groups of immigrants who began to arrive after 1898. Between 1898 and 1911 four such groups were sponsored by the government, and they formed four Chinese colonies in the First and Third Divisions of Sarawak. These groups included Hakka Christians who settled near Kuching, a large number of Foochow Methodists opening up land in the Rejang River basin, a company of Cantonese who established themselves upriver from the Foochows, and a colony of Henghuas who were given land near Sibu. In point of numbers and the subsequent success of their land and economic schemes the Foochow group was the most significant. Group immigration differed from the earlier free immigration of individuals and recruited groups in that it involved a signed contract between the Rajah and the leader or leaders who brought the agriculturists over from China with the express object of settling permanently in Sarawak on land allocated by the government. The government granted the new settlers special privileges to encourage them to concentrate their energies on agricultural activities. The leaders, also signatories to the contracts, were invariably made the headmen or *kangchews* (港主) of the settlements assigned to the groups.

The first of these groups to arrive in 1898 was composed of 100 Hakkas who had been converted to Christianity by the Basel Mission in China. They were allotted 150 acres of land three miles south of Kuching in the Sungei Maong and Batu Kawa areas and were under contract to plant padi in exchange for their land, initial financial support, and free building materials. This group soon turned their attention, however, to vegetable gardening and the breeding of domestic animals in the colony while they also engaged in other activities, including evangelization carried out among them by the Anglican Mission. For some time the Rajah was dissatisfied with this group because they did not spend their time exclusively on padi-planting. Nevertheless the colonists overcame this successfully and under their teacher, Kong Kwei En, who had come with them, they all became Anglicans. Kong grew to be a prominent member of the Kuching Chinese community. Some descendants of the original settlers still reside in the area.

The Foochows arrived in three parties after 1901 and settled in the Rejang basin near Sibu. This group was much larger than any earlier immigrant group, and their arrival was the direct result of the Rajah's enlarged plan to open up the Rejang for Chinese settlement. On 29 November 1880 he issued a proclamation in the *Sarawak Gazette* dealing with the development of the Rejang River valley. He offered to negotiate with any Chinese company that would bring into the Rejang Chinese men, women, and children numbering not less than 300 people. The settlers would be employed on the land and government offered free land sufficient for their purposes. The government also pledged to build temporary houses for the settlers and provide free rice and salt for twelve months. Communication with Kuching by steamboat was guaranteed, with the pledge of reasonable cargo rates. A police station would be built for the protection of the settlers. The latter, on their part, had to promise to settle permanently in Sarawak.

The Rajah's offer of Chinese settlement in the Rejang would not have been taken up with such enthusiasm and in so spectacular a manner had it not been for the determined efforts of Wong Nai Siong, leader of the Foochow group and founder of the Foochow community in Sarawak—a community that today, less than a century from its foundation, has outstripped almost all others in its economic potential, development capacity, and professional manpower. Wong has certainly gained for himself pride of place in Sarawak history no less than that of the early Chinese pioneers.

Wong Nai Siong was a native of Min-tsing district, in the Foochow Prefecture of Fukien Province where he was born in 1849, seven years after the signing of the Treaty of Nanking in 1842 which had forced open China's doors to foreign trade. Western influence had begun to spread steadily in China, especially in and around the treaty ports. This in turn drew zealous Christian missionaries from Western countries to come to China which they saw as a vast land of teeming millions with an ancient culture that held great promise for evangelical work. Among those who came to China were the American Methodists and they chose Foochow for their base of operations. Young Nai Siong, whose early education had been meagre, with their help and encouragement soon became a noted Chinese scholar. He passed the district level imperial examinations and was awarded the scholarly rank of *jeu-ren* (舉人) or licentiate in Chinese classics. He also became one of the Methodists' foremost converts and ardent helper. Unfortunately China at that time was at its weakest and there was great fear of foreign penetration and control. New ideas coming from the West, including Christianity, were looked upon by Chinese officials and the people alike with suspicion. The Ching dynasty, for many years, under the maladministration of the Dowager Empress Tzu Hsi, was approaching its last days since the empress held absolute power behind the dragon throne and would listen to the advice of none save those who fawned upon her and pandered to her every whim.[7] In 1898 a movement was started by a group of Chinese reformers headed by K'ang Yu-wei (康有為) with the object of introducing new measures that would modernize China. This movement had the support of the reigning emperor, Kuang Hsi, nephew of the empress, after whose installation the empress had reluctantly agreed to step down. But when the news of the reforms reached her the empress immediately re-assumed power. On her orders the emperor was imprisoned and six of the reformers were arrested and executed. Her opposition to change and her encouragement of those who were against foreign ways resulted in the uprising of the anti-foreign and anti-Christian Boxers whose avowed object was to rid China of foreign devils and Christians. Their action brought about the intervention of the combined forces of eight foreign powers which occupied Peking and Tientsin, quelled the Boxers and in 1900 compelled the empress to make peace.

Wong Nai Siong, being a Christian and having been a supporter of the reform movement,[8] was not only disillusioned by the turn of events in China but also apprehensive of his family's safety and the future of his fellow Christians in Foochow. He was a widely-travelled man and in one of his previous journeys had come to Singapore where his eldest daughter was married to Dr Lim Boon Kheng, a Straits-born Chinese physician qualified in Scotland, who in later years was to become one of the most renowned leaders of the Singapore Chinese community.[9] After the events of 1900 Wong decided to leave China for *nanyang* where he hoped to find a place to which he could lead his fellow Chinese Christians in order to settle and worship in freedom. While in Singapore with his son-in-law he learnt about Sarawak and the Rajah's plan to settle Chinese agriculturists. The Rajah's offer was a godsend to him. Taking with him an introduction from his son-in-law to Ong Tiang Swee, the Kapitan China of Sarawak, Wong visited Sarawak and was formally introduced to the Rajah with whom he subsequently concluded a thirty-one article agreement (see Appendix I), 'to introduce into the Rejang River 1,000 adult Chinese agriculturists, men, women and 300 children and to establish them in that river for the purpose of cultivating rice, vegetables, fruits, etc., but of these immigrants not more than half are to be introduced during the first year, that is to say, before June 30, 1901 . . .'.

Under the agreement the government would provide an advance of $30.00 for each adult and $10.00 for each child, two-thirds of which were to be paid through contractors in Singapore, the balance upon arrival in Kuching. The immigrants were to arrive within four months of receiving their advances in Singapore. The loan would be repaid within six years at the rate of one-fifth each year for five years. Beginning at the end of the first year, the government would pay all passages and provide not less than three acres of land for each adult, free of quit rent for twenty years, then quit rent would be collected at the rate of ten cents per acre. Compensation would be paid by the government should the need arise to re-occupy the land. The settlers were at liberty to grow and market such produce as they pleased but padi cultivation was to be the first objective. The government would construct landing stages and paths, and assist in the transportation of goods. The settlers would be given protection from any hostile or warlike natives. They might have some muskets to protect their land from the marauding wild pigs. There must be no sale of opium or gambling without permission. The government would recognize the headmen or *kangchews* recommended by the contractors; their actual duties were limited to the settlement of trivial disputes and their powers, when necessary, were to be later defined clearly. (This was in marked contrast to the almost unlimited powers given to the *kangchews* of the late nineteenth century when they were free to deal with all cases not requiring judgement in the Rajah's law courts at Kuching, and were given the opium, arrack and gambling concessions in their domains.) Finally, if all went well after two years, the same contractors could arrange for further parties of settlers, but sureties had to be given.

Wong Nai Siong obtained an initial loan of $30,000 from the Rajah and, having formed a company called Hock Long Co. with three other partners to assist him and share the cost of the venture, he set about the main business of bringing Foochow settlers from China. The first company, consisting of ninety-one people and led by Wong's partner Lek Chiang (力昌) or Lek Ngee Seng, left China towards the end of 1900 but arrived in Sarawak in January 1901 with only seventy-two, a small number having stayed behind in Singapore.[10]

The second group of 535 Foochows came in March 1901, direct from Foochow and led by Wong Nai Siong himself. The third group of 511, also led by Wong, reached Sibu in June of the following year. The new arrivals were given land at Sungei Merah (Sin Che San), several miles down the Igan River. Wong Nai Siong established an office in Sibu town for his company to deal with the affairs of the settlers. Soon a number of them moved to another area near Sibu as there was insufficient land for all the settlers at Sungei Merah. Eventually three settlements sprang up: two on the right bank of the Rejang and one on the left. Unlike the earlier Chinese who came to Sarawak, many of the Foochow settlers brought along their wives and children.

The early Foochow colonists did indeed face many hardships in the first years. The jungle was a persistent foe and much labour was needed to clear land for planting. Agricultural techniques acquired in China did not work on the tropical lowlands of Sibu. The environment was hostile. There were many insects, rats, birds, deer, and wild boar to ravage the crops, and snakes to cause havoc among domestic animals. Floods were of frequent occurrence. The low-lying swampy ground was infested with malaria and other tropical fevers and diseases. The neighbouring native tribes were often uncooperative and hostile, seeing in the newcomers foreign ursurpers of their land.

In the circumstances Wong Nai Siong found it increasingly difficult to maintain his authority among the settlers as time went on. As leader and *kangchew* of New Foochow (a name he gave to the Rejang settlement) he was personally responsible for the loans he (or his company) had obtained from the Rajah for the settlers. His company had only two active partners, himself and his assistant, Lek Chiang, who had unfortunately proved irresponsible as a leader even during the voyage of the first group of settlers.[11] Later Lek Chiang returned to China, taking with him a sum of $10,000 representing a further loan from the Rajah for recruiting more settlers. Instead of going direct to Foochow, he went to Hong Kong and Formosa.

Having exhausted his funds and falling seriously ill he finally returned to Amoy where he died. Lek Chiang's default placed an additional burden on Wong who was already heavily indebted, and raised the question of his own credibility with the Brooke administration. And, when to help him repay his debts, he resorted to a system of exacting tolls from his settlers, he got into difficulties with the Rajah's officers, although he maintained that the debts were incurred on behalf of the settlers and could therefore be recovered from them. In the end the Rajah gave Wong the option of either meeting his financial obligations or leaving the country. In 1906, five years after he had begun the Foochow settlement, Wong Nai Siong, sick and disillusioned and somewhat discredited in the eyes of the Rajah, decided to return to China.

Wong was first and foremost a scholar and knew little about farming or business management. He had grossly underestimated the hardships involved in the settlement and the vagaries of nature in a tropical rain forest. He had expected the settlers to be self-supporting in nine months, instead it took them, or those who had stayed behind, more than three years to do so. His Christian charity was responsible for the apparent lack of perception and misplaced confidence in some of his helpers and partners. Nevertheless the great work started by him was to bear fruit a decade or two later. He died in his native Min-tsing in 1924 at the age of 78, but not before he had news that his Foochow people had settled in Binatang (1908), Sarikei (1910), Song and Kanowit (1910), Baram (1920), Kapit (1921), and Sebauh (Bintulu) (1924). After Wong Nai Siong's departure from Sarawak, the Revd James Hoover, an American Methodist missionary who had been with the settlers since 1903, was appointed their new *kang-chew*. The settlement made good progress and by 1910 it was on a sound financial footing, particularly after rubber-planting which proved very profitable was taken up in 1908.

A few months after the arrival of the first group of Foochows in Sibu, two Cantonese leaders from China, Tang Kung Suk (鄧恭叔) and his partner Chiang Cho Shiong, approached the Rajah for an agreement to bring Cantonese agriculturists into other areas in the Rejang. An agreement, similar to the one Wong Nai Siong had entered into, was drawn up between the parties and signed in March 1901 (see Appendix II). The Cantonese were to be settled at Sungei Lanang, upriver from Sibu. The new concessions made by the government were that the land could be used rent free indefinitely by the settlers in return for bona fide cultivation; otherwise it would revert to government. Instead of rice, pepper was to be their chief crop. The Rajah promised help in establishing the settlers and agreed to pay $5.00 for each immigrant brought in by the leaders. The target for this settlement was 5,000 Chinese who were to come in ten annual groups of 500. The settlement was to be administered by a Chinese company which would appoint the *kangchew*. Unlike the Foochow settlement the *kangchew* of this settlement was given the right to hold farms, i.e. to sell opium and arrack or conduct gambling within the land reserve occupied by the settlers.[12] For a number of years the settlement, due to the absence of good leadership and organization, did not progress well, but by 1914 conditions improved and it extended its geographical limits from Sibu to Kanowit.

In 1911 Charles Brooke sanctioned another organized Chinese settlement scheme, also in the Rejang area, involving Henghua Methodists. Under the scheme 300 Henghuas came from Fukien under the leadership of a non-Chinese, the Revd (Dr) William Brewster, an American missionary. Land for rice cultivation was made available to the new group on the right bank of Igan River near Sungei Merah. The settlers did not seek government concessions on taxation but only asked to be given milling machinery from a recently-closed government sawmill in Kuching, and approval for the setting up of a rice company cognate to the settlement. The first 100 Henghuas of this group arrived in 1912 and immediately set to work. The land had been cleared by the time the second group came in 1913. Like the Foochows, the Henghuas were brought in to plant rice.[13] In the end they planted rubber, vegetables, and pepper besides rice. They also bred pigs and domestic birds for their own consumption and to augment their cash income. Their actions often ran counter to the stipulations of the Rajah and more than once earned his displeasure, but their efforts soon showed that by varying and diversifying their crops they had achieved a most salutary effect both on their own and the country's economy. By 1914–15 the Henghua settlement was thriving although fewer settlers than had been originally estimated had come from China to join it.

Hitherto Chinese immigrants had been brought in in large numbers only to open up land for settlement and agricultural development in the First and Third Divisions where there were large tracts of arable land readily available and where the Rajah's government had firmly established itself. The Second Division had been by-passed partly because it was mainly hilly country with poor, quartzitic soils and, unlike the First Division, lacking in mineral deposits. There the forest cover had been destroyed by generations of shifting cultivation and the rivers, elsewhere long and slow-flowing to form rich alluvial basins, are in this Division short and swift, with shallow muddy lower reaches giving rise to tidal bores in their estuaries. Also unlike the First Division where there was already settled agriculture and intensive Chinese settlement at the start of the Brooke regime, in the Second Division the Chinese population increased slowly over the years from a small number of traders who built their shops and bazaars in the protective shadow of the government forts and extended outwards from there when their numbers increased.

The extension of Chinese settlement into the Fourth Division was gradual and piecemeal. No large groups of immigrants took up land schemes in Bintulu or entered the Baram River, and the oilfields around Miri were developed with European capital. However, the success of the immigration schemes in the Rejang encouraged the Rajah to plan with the Revd James Hoover to extend similar settlement schemes to the Baram River basin. As a result twenty-five Foochows left Sibu in 1913 in a government steamer, the S.S. *L'Aubaine*, to initiate a stream of Foochow and other Chinese settlers going into the Baram area.[14] In 1923 and 1928 further Foochow communities coming from the Rejang were established at Sebauh near Bintulu and at Poyut in the Baram. Oil was discovered in Miri in 1909 and the first well was sunk in 1910. With the subsequent development of the Miri fields an influx of labour followed from other parts of the State as people began to gravitate towards the oilfields and the new town of Miri. The recruitment of skilled Chinese workmen and artisans from abroad also greatly stimulated immigration and the growth of the Chinese population in the Fourth Division.

In the Fifth Division (Limbang, Lawas, and Trusan) the early Chinese residents originated mainly from Brunei (and some from Sabah) with which it was historically linked. Their numbers were small[15] and they were chiefly engaged in trade, with investments in agricultural holdings and animal husbandry. The extraction of timber for export and the establishment of the sawmilling industry in recent years have brought about a rapid population increase, with a corresponding demand for services and skills of which the Chinese are the traditional entrepreneurs.

Chinese immigration in Sarawak continued off and on during the rule of the third Rajah, Charles Vyner Brooke (1917–41), until the Pacific War in 1941, although in later years immigrants were restricted by individual permits to relatives and dependants of those who were already established in the country.[16]

Chinese immigration in Sarawak is seen as a success story vindicating Charles Brooke's liberal land settlement policies and reflecting the ability of the Chinese entrepreneurial and planter community to provide an economic and social base, offering employment and other opportunities to the immigrants. It is at the same time the success story of the large-scale development of agriculture in Sarawak. This success is amply demonstrated by the steady growth of the Chinese population since 1871. The *Sarawak Gazette* reported in that year that an attempted census showed that of the total population of 141,546 persons the number of Chinese was 4,947, with 3,467 in Sarawak Proper. In 1877 the number had increased to 7,000 by a British estimate.[17] In 1909 Baring-Gould and Bampfylde estimated that the Sarawak Chinese numbered around 45,000. If this estimate was close it could be seen that within thirty years the Chinese community had grown seven-fold. No reliable figures for the number of Chinese between 1876 and 1939 are available. In 1939 the figure was given as 123,626, but by a government census the total Chinese population of Sarawak had increased to 145,158 out of an overall population of 546,000. In the 1959 State census the Chinese numbered 229,154. From an insignificant early number they now formed about 30 per cent of the total population. In the latest national census conducted by Malaysia in 1970 Sarawak's Chinese population was listed as 294,020, which gives a rounded 30.1 per cent of the total population of nearly one million (975,918). The rate of growth in the early years was therefore directly proportionate to the increase in Chinese immigration as related to indigenous marriages by immigrants who, prior to the implementation of group immigration schemes, invariably arrived in this country unaccompanied by their families.

1. Charles Johnson Brooke, *Ten Years in Sarawak* (London, 1886).

2. According to immigration statistics published in *Annual Reports of the Singapore Government Chinese Protectorate*, 1887–1914. After 1914 such statistics were no longer published.

3. W. J. Chater, *Sarawak Long Ago* (Kuching, BLB, 1969).

4. *Sarawak Gazette*, 20 May 1876.

5. Craig A. Lockard, 'Charles Brooke and the Foundations of the Modern Chinese Community in Sarawak, 1863–1917', *Sarawak Museum Journal*, Vol. XIX, Nos. 38–39, July–December 1971.

6. Rajah Charles Brooke's speech before Council Negri on 17 August 1915. See *Sarawak Gazette*, 1 September 1915.

7. Tzu Hsi (Yohanala) (慈禧太后) was a concubine of Emperor Han Feng (咸豐) (1851–62). Upon Han Feng's death she assisted her young

son T'ung Cher (同治) (1862–74) to ascend the throne but actually reigned in his place as empress dowager. She continued to be in control during the reign of Kuang Hsi (光緒) (1875–1908).

8. According to an autobiography published in a souvenir magazine to commemorate the Fiftieth Anniversary of the inauguration of the Sibu Foochow Settlement.

9. Dr Lim Boon Kheng, medical doctor, scholar, newspaper editor, author, Legislative Councillor (Straits Settlements), and social reformer. For an account of his life and work see Song Ong Siang's *One Hundred Years' History of Chinese in Singapore*.

10. From the reminiscences of the Revd Ting Kuang Tow (陳觀土牧師), written in 1951 for the Fiftieth Anniversary Magazine commemorating the inauguration of the Sibu Foochow Settlement. The Revd Ting came with the first group.

11. According to Revd Ting (ibid., note 10) he, two other helpers and Lek Chiang missed the first ship carrying the first group of settlers from Singapore to Kuching because Lek Chiang, who had been doing the rounds of Singapore, only arrived at the wharf after the ship had sailed.

12. The Rajah restored to the Cantonese *kangchew* the exclusive rights of *kangchews* in pepper and gambier-growing districts which had been partially withheld from the Foochow settlement. He did this perhaps out of consideration for the latter because it was a Christian settlement.

13. It is interesting to note that no signing of a land agreement was called for with the Henghua settlers.

14. *Sarawak Gazette*, 1 August 1912.

15. The Sarawak Government census of 1947 gave the breakdown figures of 1,066 men and 774 women as the total Chinese population of the Fifth Division.

16. J. R. Outram, 'Sarawak Chinese', in *The Peoples of Sarawak*, Tom Harrisson (ed.) (Sarawak Government Printing Office, 1959).

17. Spenser St. John, *Life of Sir James Brooke* (London, 1879).

7
Pre-war Social and Economic Organization

ECONOMIC POWER AND LEADERSHIP
STRUCTURE

THE processes which stimulated pre-war Chinese social and economic growth in Sarawak were many and varied, and they were all influenced by a Eurocentric colonization set in a multi-ethnic social background. It is impossible to do full justice in a single chapter to such a vast and complex subject as social and economic organization. Fortunately it is only necessary to observe those processes through issues fundamentally important in Chinese eyes in order to obtain a good perspective of how pre-war Chinese society functioned in Sarawak, and to understand why its social and economic structure has remained substantially the same until today.

Four basic issues are important to any organized society; in an overseas Chinese community they are the *raisons d'être*. These four issues are economic power, leadership structure, communal organization, and the role of education. They are here deliberately juxtaposed so as to bring out more realistically the order of their importance. It is argued that in Sarawak's Chinese society economic power is the ultimate as it determines the leadership structure, and with wealth and leadership comes the social power to further communal aims

and personal ambitions. Education, on the other hand, fur-
nishes the basic capital for the attainment of socio-economic
goals.

Economic Power

The Chinese settlers in nineteenth-century Sarawak, even
as they are today, were divided largely into two groups, rural
settlers, and town or bazaar dwellers. The rural settlers consisted mainly of miners, labourers and peasants or agriculturists, while bazaar dwellers were tradesmen, artisans and others
offering basic skills and services. For the miners and labourers
economic power was for the most part concentrated in the
kongsi and later in management or in those who offered employment. The individual agriculturists who occupied small
holdings of pepper, gambier, rubber, vegetable and food
crops had little realizable economic potential; their very existence was regulated by and often dependent on the goodwill
or co-operation of local bazaar shopkeepers and produce col-
lectors who provided them with the necessary market and
with working capital which included cash advances to finance
planting projects or to tide them over difficult periods. This
intervention of the rural bazaar shopkeepers in the basic
economy of the agriculturists formed the first link in the
chain of a multi-level credit system universally adopted by
Chinese in South-East Asia. Following the system the second
link began with the urban merchants who in their turn supplied the rural bazaar traders and agents with loan capital and
goods on credit, and directly or indirectly (that is through a
small group of well-established merchants with Singapore
connections) arranged for the export of agricultural and
native produce to Singapore and the import to Sarawak of
consumer goods and essential commodities. It was this small
but powerful group of importers and exporters who ultimately
controlled the Chinese economy in Sarawak.[1] In the middle
of the nineteenth century when the influence of the Bau
mining kongsi was at its height, Kuching Chinese merchants
were less numerous. They were comparatively ill-organized,

and the market was small. Any Chinese capital formation and accumulation was then concentrated between the aspiring urban merchants and the powerful kongsi group, with the latter setting up its own system of control over all rural shops relying upon the kongsi and its agricultural subsidiaries for patronage. After the rebellion of 1857 the base of Chinese economic power shifted from the kongsi to the merchants in Kuching, men who had shewn great loyalty to James Brooke during the rebellion and had kept Sarawak from financial disaster as the Rajah's own resources were exhausted and his political future hung in the balance. The Chinese merchants, on their side, needed the political stability of the Rajah's rule as well as well-populated, developed rural areas for the successful expansion of their trade. Mutual interest often breeds mutual dependence. It is not surprising that pioneer merchants such as Ong Ewe Hai, Chan Kho, and Law Kian Huat of that period were able to gain the Rajah's backing and patronage for building their own financial empires. In return for their services the Rajah offered them large tracts of land for the cultivation of commercial crops, encouraged them to process an old commodity, sago, into flour for the export market, and awarded them the monopoly for the farming of opium, arrack, and gambling which seemed to spring up everywhere that Chinese immigrants had settled. Eventually they also controlled labour, a commodity vital to the opening up of Sarawak's undeveloped acres. They were given the privilege of importing labourers and sponsoring immigrants from China and elsewhere in South-East Asia, both for their own agricultural and industrial projects and to work in government and private undertakings. The Rajah's fear of Sarawak's exploitation by a European planter class was an added incentive to the early Chinese merchants to consolidate and extend their economic power. The labourers and sponsored immigrants who came to Sarawak in those days were almost without exception people who belonged to the same clan and neighbourhood as the sponsors themselves. Many were even blood or clan relatives. They would be indebted both financially and socially to the sponsors who by recruiting them or sponsoring their migration had given them the opportunity to escape from the gruelling poverty, unrest, and lack of opportunity prevalent in their village or district in China. Once in Sarawak they would be obliged to take up whatever trade or occupation their sponsors had in mind for them, and accept dispersal to wherever they were told to go. Thus clan relationship, neighbourhood ties, and dialect affinity decided the occupational identification and geographical distribution of Chinese immigrants after their arrival in Sarawak. They also determined the relative position of urban and rural Chinese economy and ultimately set the pattern of Chinese society in the Sarawak context. Clan, neighbourhood, and dialect affinities were so strong that they continued for many years to permeate all sections of Chinese life. Their influence is still visible especially in traditional or family trades and professions, although beginning with the post-war period there has been a gradual change of attitude reflected by the initial acceptance of people belonging to a common surname though not of the same clan or dialect group. But as late as the 1950s it was observed that rarely would any except the largest Chinese business firms in Sarawak employ in their shops persons who, if not actually related, were not at least of the same dialect group. Clan and dialect connections also controlled occupational specialization and diversification. For example, since the early goldsmiths in Kuching were Cantonese, the goldsmiths' trade and the watchmakers' profession for a long time remained almost exclusively in Cantonese hands. Tinsmiths in Kuching and Miri were Hakkas, and Hakkas were also tailors, vegetable and pork sellers, and skilled artisans. Large-scale cabinet and furniture making was undertaken by Southern Mandarins from Kiangsu. Nearly all Sarawak's Chinese fishermen were Henghuas and they owned most of the bicycle shops and ran bus and taxi services. Catering and coffee shops were in Hainanese hands. The Luichews were engaged in the charcoal industry. Chao-ann labour controlled the ports and wharves (all above-given examples were

true except for Sibu and one or two Rejang towns in the
Third Division where most of the businesses and services were
in the hands of Foochows, Hokkiens, and some Cantonese).
Big businesses such as import and export, banking and shipping were started by Hokkiens and remained in their hands
even though other dialect groups, especially Foochow, had
entered into competition.[2]

The long and prosperous rule of Charles Brooke greatly increased the economic power of the urban merchants which
grew in direct proportion to the increase of Chinese population resulting from the implementation of liberal immigration
and land policies of the Rajah in the First and Third Divisions
of Sarawak. Chinese economic power continued to grow during the rule of the third Rajah, Charles Vyner Brooke, which
for practical purposes came to an end in 1941 with the Japanese occupation of Sarawak. Between 1857 and 1941 the
control of economic power in urban areas, First Division, rested mainly with the powerful Hokkien group of import and
export merchants already mentioned. Rural economy, on
the other hand, was largely in the hands of Teochews and
Hakkas. The Teochew community was roughly divided between trading and agriculture whereas the Hakkas were iden-
tified chiefly with sedentary agriculture. This was, however,
true only of the First and Second Divisions but not the Third
where Foochows had made large-scale settlements in the Rejang after 1901. Today the large infusion of capital and ex-
pertise from this group into big businesses, professions, and
industries all over Sarawak has seriously challenged if not
outstripped the Hokkiens in economic power. Even in the
pre-war period the Foochows were economically viable enough
to retain control of nearly all businesses and professions in
the Third Division. In the Fourth and Fifth Divisions of
Sarawak Chinese settlement began more recently. Settlers
were attracted there by the development of mineral and other
resources and by planned land settlement schemes. Economic
power in these two Divisions tended therefore to be more
evenly distributed among the diverse dialect groups of which

the settlers were composed. The controlling position thus became a prize to be won by any group or individual able to show spectacular successes in new enterprises or ventures.

Leadership Structure

The economic stratification of Sarawak's Chinese society—or alternatively the inter-relationship between rural and urban economy—is arranged like a pyramid, with a broad base of labourers and agriculturists in rural areas, a class of rural bazaar shopkeepers in the middle, and at the apex a small number of big businessmen and industrialists who actually control the economy whether in Kuching or Sibu, and who usually become the recognized leaders of the community. Whether in the pre-war or post-war period the economic strata in the Chinese community have stayed substantially unaltered. It is through this economic stratification that social power is channelled and leadership structure traditionally developed.

During the period of the Hakka kongsis in Bau, leadership rested with the heads of kongsis, supported by lesser officials who were either appointed or elected. The chief leader in each kongsi was usually a man with exceptional leadership qualities and at the same time the most influential and/or the wealthiest. This was the traditional system of leadership as practised in clan organizations in China. The members of the kongsi—the miners and agriculturists rallying around the kongsi head—would never question such leadership. It is easy to see that when a new bureaucracy of urban Chinese traders emerged after the break-up of the kongsi system to replace the old leadership, it was immediately acceptable to the Hakka rural settlers in the First Division (the traditional leadership structure of having the men with the strongest social and economic power at the top was for similar reasons acceptable to the Foochow settlers in the Third Division). Furthermore the Hakka and other agriculturists had little or no money. They needed supplies and occasionally cash loans to tide them over lean times when their rubber, pepper, or other agricultural crops failed to give them adequate returns. They could not operate without the co-operation of their nearest rural bazaar shopkeepers to whom they would be beholden and who not unnaturally exerted much influence over their lives. If we start with the rural agriculturists as the base of social power we would then find the rural bazaar shopkeepers in the position of middle rank leaders. These shopkeepers in their turn were dependent on the urban businessmen (normally also men of their own clan or dialect group) for the supply of goods on credit and as recipients of credit loans to act as agents[3] for the former in the collection of rubber, pepper, and other produce. As not all urban businessmen were also importers and exporters with large reserve capital, many would be obliged to re-direct their goods to the top Kuching merchants who, with unlimited resources and their Singapore and foreign connections, could afford to hold them in stock till marketing conditions were favourable for their export. Because of the inter-relationship between rural bazaar shopkeepers and urban businessmen as between the latter and the top merchants, it can be seen that social power was channelled through the rural shopkeepers (who derived it from the grassroots agriculturists by the granting of credits) to the urban businessmen, and again through the latter to the top merchants. Since the top merchants in Kuching were mainly Hokkiens they naturally also assumed top leadership positions.

From the beginning of Brooke rule in the 1840s the Rajah's government had always employed, for the control of the Chinese, the policy of indirect rule, that is by the appointment as official leaders of persons having or believed to have the greatest influence with the Chinese population. This policy was justified by the argument that no European could be expected to understand the complexities of Chinese society, and that provided the authorities intervened occasionally to prevent manifest abuse, the less the interference with their internal affairs the better it was for all concerned. The policy fitted in well with the traditional idea of Chinese leadership with its respect for the economically or socially powerful. This last point was amply illustrated by the fact that although the Rajah's administration maintained easy access to all races, seldom would an ordinary Chinese approach the European administrator direct, except through a Chinese intermediary generally of the leadership class, whether or not the former could speak Malay, the *lingua franca* understood by all administrators. Significantly all pre-war Chinese community leaders recognized by the Rajah's government came from the wealthy and influential merchant class or were planters who had been leaders of large migrant groups that had come to Sarawak to take up land settlement schemes. The latter were known as *kangchews* or area headmen and they had authority only over their own areas. By contrast the former leaders were given the Dutch colonial title of *Kapitan China* and their appointment conferred much power and political privilege. For example Ong Tiang Swee, the Sarawak-born son of Hokkien pioneer Ong Ewe Hai, succeeded his father as *Kapitan China* of Sarawak, an appointment which made him the paramount headman of Sarawak's Chinese community. The Rajah made him President of the Chinese Court of Justice, established in 1912 to deal with Chinese litigations, and he held that post until the court's abolition a decade later. He was made the first Chinese member of James Brooke's Supreme Council established in 1885 and later became its member for life. These were only two of the more outstanding official appointments that he held in his long and distinguished life which spanned the rule of all three Rajahs.

In the 1930s Vyner Brooke, in an endeavour to introduce improvements, established a Chinese Protectorate which later became the Secretariat for Chinese Affairs, and appointed a European civil servant with knowledge of Chinese dialects as Secretary to look after the affairs of the Chinese community, including immigration and education. To curb social abuses he promulgated laws for the protection of Chinese women and girls who were being brought into Sarawak for prostitution or for service as domestic servants. The Rajah strengthened Chinese marriage laws, making it compulsory to register marriages contracted according to established Chinese law or custom. He also set up, with Chinese subscriptions, a pauper home for the care of Chinese immigrants who were destitute or too old to work for a living and too poor to return to China. The Rajah introduced all these measures on the advice of the Secretary for Chinese Affairs who in turn had had the helpful counsel of Chinese leaders of various dialect groups, working through their respective community or clan associations and the Kuching Chinese Chamber of Commerce which had come into being at about this time.

Thus we find the pre-war Chinese leadership structure composed of an élite group of urban merchants and industrialists, supported by a broader base of middle-ranking leaders of rural bazaar shopkeepers, prominent planters and land owners, and recognized leaders of religious, civic, and social organizations. The path to leadership lay chiefly in social influence obtained through the acquisition of economic power. In other words, wealth and social power went hand in hand (as they still do). A person, financially sound or socially influential, soon gained recognition of government and reaped political privileges which in their turn brought increased wealth and prestige. The circle was complete. Conversely Chinese leadership in pre-war Sarawak did not rest on numbers; the actual preponderance of Hakkas in the First Division counted for nothing in the leadership balance. All pre-war Chinese leaders were appointed. Leadership by public consensus, i.e. by election, was not introduced till after the war.

A leadership group that derived its strength from economic power and social influence could not, of course, in a democratic sense be truly representative of Sarawak's Chinese community whose interests it was supposed to serve. But under Sarawak's peculiar system of social relationships and economic interaction between urban and rural communities this traditional form of leadership had produced positive results in the past instead of being counter-productive. It had been successful in establishing a well-ordered and prosperous Chinese society; and by individual efforts or concerted action made through community associations and the Chinese Chamber of Commerce it had brought about measures calculated to promote the social, economic, and educational welfare of the Chinese community as a whole.

COMMUNAL ORGANIZATION: THE ESTABLISHMENT OF TEMPLES, ASSOCIATIONS, AND SCHOOLS

Let us examine more closely the benefits traditional leadership had brought to the Chinese community in pre-war Sarawak, through three important aspects of communal organization: the building of places of worship, the formation of community associations, and the introduction and advancement of Chinese education.

The early Chinese immigrants to Sarawak were filled with a mixture of religious fervour and superstition. After their safe arrival in Sarawak their first thoughts were presumably to give thanks to their respective deities for protecting them on a perilous voyage, and at the same time to placate any local spirits whose territorial jurisdiction their arrival might have upset. These thoughts crystallized into the building, at first of temporary material, of a place of worship such as a shrine or a temple, to house the particular deity or deities favoured by each clan or dialect group. Later when the immigrants were well-established they would organize funds for the erection of permanent edifices. The organizers would be the same leaders who led or sponsored the migrants from China and who in the main were also the recognized leaders of their own clan groups, men of substance and influence. According to customary practice in China, a temple served not merely as a place of worship; it was equally used as a central meeting place for social activities of the clan, and for ceremonies connected with births, deaths, and marriages. In this way some temple premises in Sarawak were also used as pro-offices of the clan association or as classrooms for children before proper association or school buildings could be put up. Examples of temples so utilized were the Hok-kien Feng-shan Temple (鳳山寺), first erected in 1847, the Teochew Shang-ti Temple (玄天上帝宮), the Hainanese T'ien Hor Temple (天后廟), and the clan temple serving the three combined clan districts of Kwangtung-Hweichow-Shaoching (廣惠肇同鄉廟). All these temples are situated in Kuching. Similar temples and places of worship, though of less generous pro-portions, were built in the rural areas where immigrants began to congregate. The same urban donors, with the help of the rural community, met the cost of their erection.

After completing the place of worship the early Chinese immigrants organized themselves socially in a different man-ner. Having been uprooted from the Chinese homeland and replanted on foreign soil with its strange customs the immi-grants felt, as did other migrant groups elsewhere, the neces-sity of clinging tenaciously to the way of life that they had had to leave behind in China. This nostalgia is a common human characteristic. As soon as they were well-established the immigrants tried to satisfy this nostalgia by organizing clan associations which would bring together people of the same clan or locality in a congenial setting where they could continue familiar interests and activities. Although most clan associations began by catering for people of the same clan or neighbourhood in China, many enlarged their membership by accepting people of the same dialect group, or of the same surname although belonging to different clans and localities. These latter grew into full-fledged com-munity associations.

Clan associations helped the immigrants to strengthen group solidarity, promote understanding between members, enhance their social and economic welfare, and foster closer co-operation with other clans. They were generally able to take over diverse social roles from clan temples such as the administration of a burial ground, the organization of clan festivities, and other seasonal celebrations, thus releasing the temple premises for worship and other religious purposes. The clan association also became a venue for the distribution of charities and for alms-giving to the less fortunate members of the association and their families, the provision of accomodation and assistance to its aged and destitute; and the association's premises often served many different varieties of communal uses.

By its organizational nature a clan or community association carried on tenuous ties with the homeland. It usually came to the aid of members' families, relatives, and friends in China whenever a natural disaster struck or a civil unrest threatened, by sending funds and material for their relief and rehabilitation. Cultural ties were maintained with China by the recruitment and appointment of scholars from the same clan or locality to teach in schools under its aegis. Civil or political instability in China had always been one of the main causes of Chinese emigrating overseas. It was hardly surprising that all immigrants felt deep and abiding concern about events in China, especially in their home districts. Even successive generations of Sarawak-born Chinese who still retain the traditional way of life felt the same interest. As a rule this lay dormant but was quickly translated into action when China's territorial integrity or national life was threatened; for example, in the 1930s Japan perpetrated unprovoked aggression on China in a series of military 'incidents' with the object of conquest and colonization. The Chinese community in Sarawak, together with other Chinese communities in South-East Asia, reacted immediately with various measures, including the establishment of a State-wide China Relief Fund to raise money for the refugees and to contribute towards the cost of passages for volunteer technicians and drivers who returned for service in China. Action to help China's war effort was taken through community associations working under the direction of the Kuching Chinese General Chamber of Commerce. Work of the China Relief Fund was continued until the Japanese occupation of Sarawak in 1941.

In this way the community associations could be said to involve themselves in active politics, but their political involvement concerned the Chinese mainland, with which they had a slight but necessary connection, not Sarawak where the Chinese community had always been loyal to the Rajah's government. The Chinese community's involvement in the war effort also had the tacit encouragement of the government since part of the funds raised went towards the British War Effort after the Second World War started in 1939 when Japan became the common foe of both China and Britain. Furthermore, with the Brooke policy of indirect rule there had never been active interference in matters concerned only with China and not detrimental to Sarawak's interests. This had been clearly shown when Rajah Charles Brooke took no steps in 1911 or 1912 to prevent political agents of Dr Sun Yat Sen, leader of the Chinese Nationalist Revolutionary Party which overthrew the Manchu imperial government, coming to Sarawak to collect funds and recruit men for his party, or to dissolve or proscribe a branch of the party, called the Chinese People's Association (國民社), set up in Bau to further its cause.[4] By 1941 most of the Chinese community associations in Kuching, as we know them today, were in existence.[5] The majority of those formed after the war were in the Third and other Divisions. According to the law in force at the time only associations, societies, and clubs with a membership of more than ten members needed to notify government of their existence. No registration was necessary.

Given below is a list of the older associations, the first was established in 1853 and the last in 1936. Nearly all are in Kuching.

Kong-Wei-Shiu (Kwangtung-Hweichow-Shaoching)
    Association (廣惠肇公會), established 1853
Teochew Association (潮州公會), 1864
Hokkien Association (福建公會), 1871
Kaying (Five Common Clans) Association (嘉應五屬同鄉會),
    1881
Khengchew (Hainanese) Association (瓊州公會), 1898
T'aipu Clan Association (大埔同鄉會), 1920
Foochow Association (Sibu) (福州公會), 1930

  Hakka Community Association (客屬公會), 1934
  Chao-Ann Association (詔安會舘), 1936
  Luiyang (Luichew) Association (雷陽會舘), 1936
  This list does not take into account Chinese Chambers of Commerce, Benevolent Societies, etc., which had increased in number by 1941. The oldest Benevolent Society was presumably Sibu's Foochow Kong Yan Society(光遠慈善社) established in 1910. In 1930 the Kuching Chinese General Chamber of Commerce (古晋中華總商會) was established through the efforts of Hokkien community leaders.

ROLE OF EDUCATION, WITH A PERSPECTIVE OF CHINESE AND ENGLISH EDUCATIONAL SYSTEMS

Education is perhaps the most important aspect in the communal organization of the Chinese in Sarawak, since education determines not only the present roles but the future shape and content of Chinese society in relation to others. Thus it is, and has always been, a matter of pivotal concern to the Chinese community. The early Chinese pioneers were generally men with little or no formal education, whether farmers or traders, and they had to rely on a few men of letters for all their needs. Like their counterparts in China the scholars commanded high respect and were classified with the leaders whose advisers they often became. But their own lack of learning was a constant reminder to the immigrants, irrespective of their social status, that they must give their children a good education, whatever the cost. Urban merchants and clan leaders with their wealth could afford to engage or import scholars from China as tutors for their children, although they were prepared to extend the service to children of their associates, friends, and acquaintances. The clan temple, being communal property, was often 'borrowed' for use as a classroom. There was normally only one teacher and he taught Chinese classics. Learning was by rote and constant repetition, and strict discipline was enforced by 'birching'. This sytem of *sze-su* (私塾) or private tutoring was universally followed in the nineteenth century, and in Sarawak, as elsewhere in South-East Asia, it became the forerunner of the Chinese school system. As the numbers increased and more facilities were needed for the pupils, the clan leaders, around whom the Chinese community revolved, got together to plan the building of proper schools with a large staff, and to organize fund-raising campaigns for this purpose. The most generous donors and active organizers were naturally the same leaders. In the rural areas the story was somewhat different, but there was no question of setting back the determination of even the poorest Chinese labourer or farmer to educate his children. Those who lived close to the towns would send their children to schools sponsored by community associations; this they often did at great personal sacrifice to themselves. Others in remote rural districts solved the problem of establishing rural schools by seeking the patronage of middle-rank leaders—the area headmen, the *Kapitans China*, and the well-to-do rural bazaar shopkeepers (and through them large donations were frequently obtained from the affluent urban merchants and other wealthy persons), who for prestige and other reasons were usually ready to play a leading role in such projects. The rural farmers made up for their poor pecuniary support by offering free labour for site preparation and work on the school premises. Unlike schools in the towns which began as clan schools, those in rural areas started well as community schools catering for children of all neighbouring Chinese residents.

Chinese schools in pre-war days were public schools, that is they were established by public funds from the Chinese community and were managed by their own school boards. Finance for the schools was guaranteed by the clan or community associations, supplemented where necessary by public subscriptions. Some of the schools were fee-paying; others were styled 'free' schools, but most ended up by charging small fees while reserving a percentage of free places for the genuinely poor but brilliant pupils. The richer associations later offered scholarship grants to enable the best pupils to further their academic careers.[6] The larger schools even provided bilingual curricula, teaching both Chinese and English (for example, the Hokkien Free School); and nearly every urban Chinese school taught a little English as a subject. By 1941 the Chinese school system had spread to all districts in Sarawak and hundreds of Chinese schools were scattered over the country, forming a network with schools in areas with sizeable Chinese populations. The schools in urban Kuching, Sibu, and Miri had brought their academic standards pre-war up to the Junior Middle or *Tzu-chung* (初中) level, while those in the rural areas had reached the Higher Primary Standard or *Kao-shio* (高小).

In urban areas the school board members were invariably clan or community leaders or those recognized by the administration who were also officials of their respective associations. As these leaders were persons of means and social position it was their support that kept the urban schools going and improving their academic performance. By contrast the rural school boards consisted of area headmen and rural bazaar shopkeepers, with a sprinkling of well-to-do planters and farmers.

Unlike the old Chinese scholars of the nineteenth century, under the system of community schools teachers became paid employees of the school board or the community association which had the power to employ or dismiss them. Their employment was on a contract basis, terminable upon its expiry or on good cause shown. Apart from fixed salaries and free accommodation provided by the school there were few other employment benefits, such as superannuation payments. In short, school teachers were regarded as hired professionals and they no longer enjoyed the traditional respect due to scholars. The renewal or otherwise of their teaching agreements thus depended entirely on the kind of relationship that teachers were able to maintain with the school board on one side and the pupils as well as their parents on the other. In other words, teaching in Chinese schools in those days depended on patronage as much as did other professions. This was understandably a source of great dissatisfaction to Chinese school teachers, especially those in rural areas where members of the school board also controlled the local economy. The latter's prestigious position made them the underwriters of the local schools and sole arbiters over teachers' appointments or dismissals. It gave them the 'prerogative' to impose their dominant views on school management and to interfere in matters traditionally within the province of the teaching profession.

Until the Japanese occupation Sarawak's Chinese schools were conducted on a dialect group basis. Thus the Hokkien School in Kuching served the Hokkien community, Min Teck School the Teochew, Yueh Kwang School the Hakka community; and in Sibu the Chung Hua and other schools served the Foochow community, and so on. In practice, however, all Chinese schools in pre-war days kept a certain percentage of places available to students from other dialect groups so long as they were Chinese. Exceptional students from other racial groups were admitted. After the introduction of Mandarin as the common medium of instruction in all schools in the 1930s the system of dialect grouping served only the convenience of financial and administrative control rather than as a pointer for the selection and admission of students.

A reference table containing the names of Chinese schools established in Kuching, First Division (with a few in the Third Division) in the early decades of the twentieth century is included (see p. 88). Details of schools in rural areas in the First and other Divisions of Sarawak are unfortunately not available.

The basic difference between the schools in the First and the Third Divisions was that whereas the former (1—7) had all been established by or under clan or community associations, the latter (8—12) were the result of efforts by individual educationists in the Foochow settlements.

Chinese education was not the only medium available to

Locality	Name of School	Year of Establishment	Established by
1. Kuching	Hokkien Free School (福建義務學校)	1912	Hokkien Association
2. Kuching	Min Teck School (民德學校)	1916	Teochew Association
3. Kuching	Yik Kuan School (益群學校)	1918	Kong-Wei-Shiu Association
4. Kuching	T'ai Tung School (大同學校)	1923	Taipu Association
5. Kuching	Kung Min School (公民學校)	?	Kaying Association

(Nos. 4 and 5 were combined in 1936 to form the Yueh Kwang School (越光學校) for Hakkas.)

6. Kuching	Yueh Kwang School (越光學校)	1936	Hakka Community Association
7. Kuching	Chung Poon School (崇本學校)	?	Khengchew (Hainan) Association
8. Sibu	Chung Cheng School (中正中小學)	1906	Private Individuals
9. Sibu	Chung Hua School (中華中小學)	1907	Private Individuals
10. Kanowit	Khi Ting Primary School (沂亭小學)	1919	Private Individuals
11. Binatang	Kai Wen School (開文中小學)	1922	Private Individuals
12. Sarikei	Sze Mei School (泗美小學)	1925	Private Individuals

the Sarawak Chinese. European Missionary societies began to establish themselves in the country soon after James Brooke had stabilized his rule. The Rajah not only welcomed them and their good influence among the populace but they also became his allies. Charles Brooke was a keen educationist and he opened two vernacular schools which taught Chinese in Upper Sarawak in 1902 and later provided a High School for boys of all races in Kuching, teaching both English and Malay.[7] He gave the Missions his continued support to extend their activities and granted small subsidies to their schools. The first of such Missionary Societies to arrive in Kuching in 1848 was the Society for the Propagation of the Gospel (SPG), an Anglican organization. This society was later known as the Anglican Church of Borneo. The Roman Catholic Mission, starting also in Kuching, came in 1881, to be followed in 1903 by the Methodist Episcopal Church after Wong Nai Siong and his fellow Foochow Christians had established land settlements in the Rejang in 1901. The Seventh Day Adventist Mission was the last to arrive before the war. All Missionary Societies had the common aim of bringing Christianity and its message of goodwill and brotherly love to the many races in Sarawak. The missionaries did this not only by building churches and places of worship and by spreading Christian teachings in different ways, but they also offered many social and humanitarian services to the people by establishing orphanages, welfare homes, medical clinics, and hospitals. These services are still continued, but it is in education that they have made the most signal contribution. The missionaries were dedicated educationists and teachers. They conducted schools mainly in English,[8] the language of the rulers and the administration, which were the first to give the young of Sarawak's multi-racial population an opportunity to acquire a sound formal education. Although such schools were open to pupils of all religious faiths and races, it soon became obvious that they attracted chiefly local-born Chinese boys. This happened despite the fact that the Sarawak Chinese community in those days was traditionally Buddhist and that it had shown a firm preference for its own language and culture. The explanation was perhaps the overriding Chinese love of education for its own sake. Also, by sending their children to learn the language and customs of the rulers, Chinese parents might find new opportunities open to them and their offspring in commerce and in the administration. It is important to note this choice of Chinese parents to send their children to English-medium schools because their decision was to split Sarawak's educated Chinese into two camps, often opposed to each other in views and outlook as well as in aims and beliefs. Economically and socially the split also created two distinct groups with a wide social distance between them.

The mission schools were very successful owing to the dedication of their teachers and the support of both government and the public, and also because of the high standards of education maintained by them and constantly improved upon. Long before 1941 the two principal boys' schools, St Thomas's of the Anglican Mission and St Joseph's of the Roman Catholic Mission, both in Kuching (later with their counterparts for girls), became the main sources of recruitment to staff the local civil and other public services of the Rajah's government at different levels. This was followed by the Methodist and other missionary schools. English-educated Chinese, both Christian and non-Christian, thus accounted for a good percentage of Sarawak's civil servants before the war who, together with colleagues of other races, kept the Rajah's administrative machinery running smoothly. English-educated Chinese from mission schools also entered the teaching and other professions or worked in European-owned commercial houses and banks. Others joined their peers from Chinese schools in the business world, but those who did so were more likely to be sons or relatives of Chinese merchants and tradesmen who already had a traditional business background. Knowledge of English would give this type of young businessmen a chance to break into the international market.

Thus in pre-war Sarawak two systems of education existed for the benefit of the Chinese community: the Chinese-medium schools, supported and financed by the community itself through its associations; the English-medium schools conducted by Missionary Societies. Owing to the basic differences between the two systems a wide social gulf existed between their products. There were differences not only in the knowledge and application of the languages they had learnt but also in their outlook and approach to life, in their choice of occupation, and often in their beliefs and loyalties. Someone crudely labelled the Chinese-educated as China-oriented and the English-educated as England-oriented. This is, of course, an over-simplification. The differences were caused as much by social, economic, and political factors as by divergences in their educational background. For example, a school leaver with a Junior Middle Three Certificate from a Chinese school in pre-war Sarawak (the equivalent of the English Overseas Cambridge Junior School Certificate, both being the highest academic levels reached by the two different systems up to 1941) had only one or two avenues open to him in choosing an occupation. He could be a businessman if he had the capital or the right connections, or he could become a Chinese-school teacher in a rural school—untrained, of course, because formal training of teachers did not begin till after the war. Failing these he might be forced by circumstances to become an artisan, a mechanic, or a skilled workman. If he came from the rural areas he might have to return to his parents' farm, but he would do so without enthusiasm since his parents had expected greater things of him by making sacrifices to give him a secondary education. For him to land a government job was out of the question because Chinese-school qualifications were not recognized by the government. In any case, he would know little English and would not even be considered. By contrast his counterpart from an English-medium school would have a recognized certificate, even if at a junior secondary level. He could apply to become a clerk or even an executive in the Sarawak public service, or in a European firm or bank, or he could join the teaching profession. If he showed ability he could steadily rise to more senior positions. Socially and financially he was considered to be a cut above his Chinese-educated counterpart, and he commanded respect even among the community leaders and other people of social prominence, especially if he worked directly under European officers of senior rank who were in a position to grant social privileges.

Little wonder that such a wide gulf existed between the products of the two different systems or that there was practically no social communication between them. There was indeed an in-between group consisting of those who had received a bilingual education and who could bridge the gap, but their number was small and there was an unfortunate tendency for them to become completely western or completely Chinese in their manner of life if they had acquired a good higher education. As was to be expected there were feelings of jealousy and discontent as well as resentment from the Chinese-educated group towards their English-educated counterparts, disguised by an over-advocacy to return to everything Chinese and the condemnation of those who considered Western education and way of life superior to others. This resentment was not, however, directed solely at the English-educated or at a government that did almost nothing for those who chose to be educated in their own language, but increasingly also at the traditional community leaders and others who, whilst actively promoting Chinese education and culture, showed their own preference for sending their children to English-medium schools. There was also much discontent even among the Chinese-educated because those who had wealthy connections soon realized their goals and rose to social prominence, whereas the bright but poor lads who came from humble homes and could find no patronage might fail for years to obtain satisfactory employment. This was especially the case with rural young Chinese who were handicapped from the beginning by a generally lower school education (since nearly all the rural Chinese schools pre-war offered education up to the Higher Primary level only). They, like their urban counterparts, had gone to school in the hope of being able to quit the life of toil to which their illiterate parents were condemned; instead they found that without a good education and lacking help from people with social influence, even average skilled jobs were difficult to find. Even if they wished to return to the soil as educated farmers they would require capital and perhaps more land, and access to both would be almost impossible to obtain without patronage.

In order to understand why in Sarawak in the post-war colonial period and immediately after the formation of Malaysia there was mounting communist activity reaching the point of armed struggle; and increased support for radical political solutions to social and economic problems advocated by the communist organization, it is necessary to realize that the seeds of insurgency had already been sown in pre-war years. By an autocratic system of government that largely ignored the Chinese masses (except where they were economically indispensable) and their social, economic, and educational problems; by perpetuating indirect rule through an élite ruling class of their own countrymen with which they were disenchanted, and by continuing to grant privileged status to the English-educated in employment situations, the way was being gradually but inexorably prepared for drastic change. Matters were not helped by nearly five years of Japanese occupation and domination which taught young Chinese independence of action for survival. In addition, the infiltration of communist ideology into Chinese schools and Chinese society, aided and abetted by those already disillusioned by the existing social order, prepared the way for the course of events which naturally followed.

1. Dr J. K. T'ien gave the number of this small group as 9 in 1948 of which 5 were Hokkiens, 3 Teochews and 1 Hakka. They were all linked with Singapore firms of the same dialect group; 5 were actually branches of Singapore firms, the other 4 acted as commission agents. In Sarawak the big nine also dealt with or through European firms such as the Borneo Co. or Sime Darby. The balance of economic power as well as the dialect composition of this group was altered in recent years with the emergence of the economically powerful Foochow group, although the Foochows, being from Fukien Province, are broadly regarded as Hokkiens (Cf. *The Chinese of Sarawak, A Study of Social Structure*, London School of Economics and Political Sciences Monograph series, 1953).

2. J. R. Outram, 'Sarawak Chinese' from Tom Harrisson (ed.), *The Peoples of Sarawak*. This was the position in the 1950s and pre-war.

Since then social and political changes, dictated by a changed economy, have distributed occupational specialization more evenly among the various dialect groups.

3. Not strictly in the agency sense of receiving a commission but the rural bazaar shopkeepers would purchase or collect rubber, pepper, and other produce from the farmers and producers for re-sale to the urban merchants for export to Singapore.

4. This information was gleaned from records kept by the writer's father who was one of the association's officials.

5. A 1947 analysis shows a total of 156 Chinese associations in existence in Sarawak, see *Sarawak Government Gazette*, 1 October 1947.

6. By 1979 well-established Chinese community associations in Sarawak yearly offered a number of scholarships, mostly local, but a few do extend to tertiary education abroad.

7. Baring-Gould and Bampfylde, *History of Sarawak under its Two White Rajahs*, chapter XVII. These schools appear to have closed down after a while. No other information about them is available.

8. The Missionary Societies also provided Chinese-medium schools in the First and Third Divisions. In the latter these schools constitute a special feature of Chinese education in Sarawak.

8

The Japanese Occupation and After

THE Second World War broke out in the autumn of 1939 when Hitler's armies marched into Poland, and Britain and France declared war on Germany. Soon the war spread to most parts of Europe. As in the First World War of 1914–18 Sarawak was not directly involved in the European conflict but the Chinese community, together with the European and other communities, was engaged in many different efforts to raise funds which were shared between British War Funds and the China Relief Fund, the latter being remitted to China for the relief and rehabilitation of refugees in consequence of the Sino-Japanese war which had begun in 1937. But when Japan signed new military pacts with Germany and Italy to form the Axis alliance and Britain and her allies were involved in the Western theatre of war, there was increasing fear that Sarawak, together with the rest of South-East Asia, might be directly threatened by a Japanese invasion.

In March 1941, Rajah Charles Vyner Brooke proclaimed his intention to end the absolute rule of his family and replace it by a form of government with wider participation which would gradually prepare the people for self-government. A new constitution to bring about this change came into effect in September 1941. Under this constitution the Rajah reorganized the Council Negri or State Council, and for the first time officially appointed four Chinese representatives to it.[1] Before this, and since 1937, two prominent Chinese, Ong Tiang Swee, a life member of the Supreme Council, and Wee Kheng Chiang, one of the Rajah's Chinese advisers and Chairman of the Chinese General Chamber of Commerce, had attended the Council's meetings on invitation. Except for the dubious distinction of having four appointed Chinese members to represent the Chinese on the Council instead of two who were there by invitation, the Chinese community as a whole benefited little from the Rajah's constitutional exercise. However, the Chinese were appreciative of the prosperity and progress that a hundred years of stable Brooke rule had brought to their community, and so they excelled themselves in organizing with other communities in September 1941 mammoth celebrations throughout Sarawak to commemorate James Brooke's accession to the Raj on 24 September 1841.

The war clouds which had been gathering in the Pacific burst on 7 December 1941 when Japan attacked Pearl Harbor in Hawaii and thus brought America into the war. The Japanese forces moved swiftly. Radiating from Camranh Bay in Vietnam in several pincer movements their naval units separately landed at Kota Bharu and Singora on the east coast of Malaya (now West Malaysia) on 7 and 8 December and by 16 December their troops were already in occupation of the oilfields in Miri and Seria. On Christmas Eve, 24 December 1941, the Japanese landed off Pending in Kuching after their aircraft had strafed and bombed Kuching town on the 19th. Christmas Day saw the invading armies in full possession of the town. Sibu, the chief town of the Third Division, fell on 29 December. Thus began a military occupation of Sarawak which was to last till 15 August 1945 when Japan surrendered to the Allied powers.

The Japanese swept on to engulf much of Borneo and many of the neighbouring islands before February of the following year. Their dash down the Malay Peninsula ended with the capture of heavily-fortified Singapore on 15 February. Although the Japanese invasion was expected in Sarawak no one seemed to have anticipated the speed of their advance. According to the military plans for Sarawak, closely guarded secrets at the time,[2] there would be no defence of North Borneo (Sabah), Brunei, or Labuan as the forces available were inadequate and the oilfield installations and refinery at Miri, Seria, and Lutong would be rendered useless, but the Kuching area, because of the airfield and the access it provided to the Dutch airfield in Singkawang about sixty miles south-east of Kuching, would be defended. The plan was revised after an Anglo-Dutch conference in September which decided that no attempt would be made to defend Kuching but that only static defence would be conducted around the airfield and at strategic points by the small detachments of 2/15 Punjabi Regiment, the only regiment sent by Britain for the protection of Sarawak in honour of the agreement of 1888. In the event, very little resistance was offered to the invaders. A contingency plan to evacuate the European community and British civil service personnel was launched too late. Very few escaped successfully and the majority were interned as prisoners-of-war.

With the occupation of Sarawak by the Japanese the Chinese and other ethnic groups were at their mercy. For the Chinese community there was good reason for fear and trepidation because Japan and China were at war and the Japanese were regarded as enemies by all Chinese and vice versa. Community leaders who had helped to organize the civil defence services and in fund-raising projects feared Japanese reprisals on two counts: for siding with the British and their cause, and for showing loyalty to China by boycotting the sale of Japanese goods. They had also sent money to China (through the China Relief Fund) as well as volunteer drivers, etc., to aid the Nationalist Government in their fight against the Japanese. Young Chinese were afraid lest the Japanese, who had conscripted Taiwanese and Koreans to fight their war, were also going to impose conscription or recruit forced labour in

Sarawak; their womenfolk were petrified by the stories of massacre, rape, physical assault, and other atrocities that the Japanese soldiers were reported to have perpetrated in China.

In these circumstances the only possible relationship between the Chinese and the Japanese was that of victors and vanquished. Fortunately for all communities, because the occupation of Sarawak was accomplished at minimal cost to the Japanese and because the population, on the whole, was not hostile, there was little reason for the conquerors to begin a campaign of oppression, even of the Chinese. Within a few days of their occupation the Japanese set up a Gunseibo (軍政部) or Military Administration in Kuching and subsequently in the other chief towns and recalled a number of local civil servants, Chinese among them, to assist in restoring some form of civil government. Recognized Chinese community leaders and others were sent for and requested to relay the Japanese military's orders and directives to the people. There were various attempts to win over the latter by propaganda and other forms of inducement. Rally meetings were held and huge posters displayed to explain to all races that Japan had no colonial ambitions but that they were taking over Sarawak and other South-East Asian territories solely to help the oppressed peoples get rid of Western colonial control, and to form with neighbourly Japan a region of economic co-operation to be known as the 'Greater East Asia Co-prosperity Sphere' (大東亞共榮圈). In spite of these attempts the Sarawak Chinese tried as far as possible to keep their distance. Young men not engaged in essential work in the towns soon 'disappeared' into the country, ostensibly to carry out the Japanese administration's exhortations to plant more food crops, but in reality to avoid being recruited into the *kyodo-hei* (郷土兵) or local army corps which the Japanese, as expected, soon began to organize, or being deployed in labour squads formed to work at the 7th Mile aerodrome or in building new airstrips and boat-building yards. The *kyodo-heis* were trained for local defence and supplemented the police force and the *kempetai* (憲兵隊) or military police in keeping law and order.

The work of the labour squads was very important and dangerous, especially in the later stages of the war when Allied air and naval activity was intensified. Young Chinese girls of marriageable age were dispersed to the countryside to join their relatives and friends; those that had no such connections were persuaded to marry, sometimes men who were total strangers and whose qualities were unknown, to avoid falling into the hands of unscrupulous brothel-keepers who were recruiting girls to entertain the troops.

Although there was no actual persecution the Japanese did not let off the Chinese lightly either. Soon after the occupation a number of Chinese leaders, school teachers, and intellectuals in Kuching and other main towns of Sarawak, who had taken part in raising funds for China's refugees or were on suspicion of being anti-Japanese, were arrested, detained and tortured by the *kempetai*. A few lost their lives as a result of the torture or were executed; the lucky ones escaped with imprisonment (after military courts had been set up with Japanese judges) of varying lengths. The ordinary Chinese in the lower strata of society—junior civil servants, teachers, commercial employees, tradesmen, etc.—were enrolled in special classes set up by the army to learn Japanese; they also had to attend rallies and civic sessions arranged for their benefit.

Chinese traders whose businesses offered a service considered essential to the occupation forces and the local people were permitted to continue, but their business were placed under stringent control to ensure priority of supply to the military. Strict food rationing was soon introduced as Allied attacks on Japanese shipping were disrupting supplies. The Japanese meted out severe punishment for profiteering and black market activities. By the second half of the occupation period most of the Chinese shops were closed for lack of goods and their owners and shop workers soon left to take up farming in rural areas. Some, in spite of the risks involved, carried on in the black market. As supplies became more scarce smuggling of food and essential commodities became a common way of life. Chinese farmers, feeding off the land, found themselves better off than their urban fellow-countrymen.

All the non-essential public services were discontinued under the military occupation. Schools were closed except for those converted into centres for teaching Japanese. English was prohibited though Malay was used as it provided a common medium of communication. Chinese was discouraged and Chinese schools, with their traditional school boards, were regarded with disfavour. Chinese community associations were either closed or existed only in name, their traditional roles looked upon with suspicion. However, like all foreign victors the Japanese suffered from lack of effective liaison with the people. After the initial period of harshness they began to reinstate a large number of old leaders and to appoint new men who were prepared to co-operate in assisting them to control the Chinese. A few former Chinese leaders, men of high principles and loyal both to their own people and the Brooke administration, strove by all possible means to avoid reinstatement, but the majority felt that they had no choice but to work with the Japanese. Whatever the extenuating circumstances, in the eyes of the Chinese community these leaders were collaborators with the enemy. Since China and Japan were at war any friendly gesture towards the Japanese was considered an intolerable offence. The misbehaviour of the Chinese leaders who co-operated with the Japanese was to have a profound psychological effect on the future Chinese leadership. Before the occupation the Chinese public were content to regard their leaders as leaders despite their faults. Now the acknowledged leadership had been tested and found wanting. Unfortunately, too, the colonial government in Sarawak later ill-advisedly restored most of the collaborators to their former positions, an act the Chinese public considered most unbecoming. Henceforth they were determined more to rely on their own resources than trust such leaders; at best they were wary of trusting any except those who redeemed themselves by advancing public interests rather than their own. This change of attitude gradually resulted in a shift from traditional leadership to a group of rising leaders, young intellectuals with mainly Chinese educational background, who were willing to serve the people although their social and political views tended towards the left. The emergence of this new leadership was to influence to a great extent the political thinking of the Chinese and change the expression of Chinese politics in the years ahead.

EARLY POST-WAR YEARS AND COLONIAL RULE

The military occupation of Sarawak formally ended on 11 September 1945 when Australian forces entered Kuching to receive the Japanese surrender. Soon after this the British Borneo Civil Administration Unit (BBCAU), a unit of the British Military Administration, took over the administration of the country pending Rajah Vyner Brooke's return to resume the reins of government. During nearly five years of occupation Sarawak had suffered great devastation, not so much in the material sense as in an almost complete breakdown of the country's economy. Trade was disorganized; food, clothing, medicine, and other daily necessities were all in short supply. Production of rubber, pepper, and other export crops on which Sarawak had depended virtually ceased, and the Japanese had destroyed the Miri oilfields just before their surrender. There was a backlog of social problems arising from the closure of schools and the denial to the people of a normal way of life.

The Chinese community, in conjunction with others, had hoped that with peace restored Vyner Brooke would soon return to rally his Sarawak subjects and set the country on the road to recovery. And so when in April 1946, he did arrive in Sarawak and the BMA handed back to him the civil government there was rejoicing. But the Rajah soon let it be known that he wished to cede Sarawak to Britain as a colony. He intended to do so for several reasons, the cogent one being that Sarawak was too poor to recover on its own. By ceding it to the British crown he was thinking of the country's best interests, because Britain had the finance, the technical knowledge, and the necessary experience to develop Sarawak into a modern state. The Rajah's Private Secretary travelled over Sarawak to explain his wishes. Two Malay-speaking members of Parliament came from Britain to gauge the people's reaction to the cession proposal. Feelings ran high; the country was soon divided into two opposing camps, one for and one against cession. Even the Rajah's own family was split by differences of opinion.[3]

The Cession Bill was brought to a special session of Council Negri for debate, and was finally passed at its second reading on 17 May 1946 by a narrow margin of nineteen votes for and sixteen votes against. Generally speaking the Malays, who had enjoyed much political advantage under Brooke rule, were against cession, seeing in it the loss of a privileged position. The Dayaks and other native races wanted more time in which to make up their minds, but they would follow the Rajah's judgement. The European members who were mostly the Rajah's officers (and were given leave to vote according to their conscience) were divided in their views. The Chinese were mainly in favour of cession as they saw in it financial and educational benefits and technical advance which Britain's huge resources were able to provide for Sarawak. The Chinese mood was reflected in a speech made by Kho Peng Loong, Third Division representative, who said:

> As I am a representative of the Chinese in the Rejang River district, I give my support to the cession, for under British rule the two main vices of gambling and opium-smoking will be abolished and the status of the Chinese will be raised to the same position as that of the natives of Sarawak. Under the British rule there will be better education, better agriculture and faster development of the country to the general advantage of all the people in the country.[4]

The Chinese attitude over the cession issue was not difficult to surmise. The Brooke regime had opened Sarawak to Chinese settlement and trade, it is true, and its stable government had encouraged Chinese population growth and the expansion of its economy. Of these benefits they were appreciative; but they also realized that they were not recognized, even the new generations born and bred on Sarawak soil, as true sons of the soil or natives which was (and still is) a privileged position without carrying the pejorative connotation so common elsewhere in Asia and Africa under colonial rule. Until 1931, a Chinese could legally be classified as a native, but the classification denoted nationality rather than ethnic status. After 1931 Chinese and non-Islamic Indians were excluded from native status. This was underlined in the Land Rules of 1933.[5]

There had been no real attempts to understand the Chinese. Because of indirect rule most contacts with the Chinese had always been made through a small group of privileged Chinese leaders who traditionally belonged to the wealthy and influential merchant class, or were appointed area headmen and *kapitans*, and through the European and Asian members of the Sarawak civil service. The Rajahs had respected the Chinese for their industry but had also been suspicious of their activities and intentions, which no doubt arose out of mutual ignorance and common disdain for each other's way of life. After the rebellion of 1857 and the break-up of the Bau kongsi James Brooke's government passed a law in 1870 which imposed the death penalty on a leader of a secret society and severe punishment on its membership. The resultant social vacuum and organizational void was filled by the Chinese with multi-purpose clan, dialect, and communal organizations which in the twentieth century built up towards an apex represented by the Chinese Chamber of Commerce. The Chamber was established by the wealthy merchants who were also the recognized community leaders, and was regarded by the government as the official organ and mouth-piece of the Chinese community. Whilst the Chamber had strengthened the powers of traditional leadership it did nothing to inculcate among the Chinese a civic consciousness or sense of belonging to their country of adoption, thus altering their habitual clinging to ways of life of the old country. It was therefore not surprising to find the Chinese community, as a whole, still looking to China with more concern about the events and political changes taking place there than happenings in Sarawak. This pre-occupation with their motherland found expression in increased efforts to send aid to China in times of need, etc. and in viewing local events through singularly China-focused eyes. It also created a general attitude which non-Chinese usually interpreted as indifference—an attitude which seemed unconcerned with who formed the government but whether that government's policies would be favourable or not to Chinese interests.

As generally anticipated, Britain's taking over of Sarawak as a Crown colony did benefit all races, not least the Chinese. Whilst preserving Sarawak's old but beneficial customs and practices and maintaining the privileged position of natives over land rights and other customary matters, the colonial administration increased the pace of development in the economic, social, and educational fields in order to hasten the process of self-government leading eventually to independence. This fulfilled a pledge Britain had made when the Rajah handed over Sarawak's territory to the British Crown. To achieve this goal much money was needed, and massive financial aid was given in the immediate post-war years by Britain under the Colonial Development and Welfare Fund for the construction of infra-structure such as radio communications, roads, ports, and airfields and the building of schools, training colleges, and hospitals. All these projects benefited different ethnic groups. Aid was specially given to develop the rural economy by subsidizing projects covering improved padi and rubber cultivation and pepper planting. The rural agricultural schemes were of special benefit to thousands of Chinese planters and farmers who lived in the country. In the urban centres the Chinese economic community, perhaps the hardest hit by the occupation, was, under colonial administration, soon able to recover, and the task was made easier by the industrial boom experienced by the manufacturing countries after the war, resulting in high prices being paid for pepper, rubber, and other raw materials that Sarawak produced. The high price of pepper, for example, enabled a good number of Hakka agriculturists who owned large pepper plantations in the First Division to accumulate enough capital to purchase shop-houses in the urban areas, and so to change their occupation to that of traders and merchants. With the boom in the prices of rubber and pepper the urban merchants made good profits as wholesale exporters and importers. This in turn made it possible for them to finance new business ventures such as shipping, transport, banking, and the manufacture of consumer goods. An active Chinese community, the Foochows of the Third Division, obtained timber concessions and entered whole-heartedly into the logging and sawn timber business which in that Division used to be the preserve of Hokkiens. So prosperous have they become that today they vie with the leading Hokkien community and foreign commercial houses and banks in successfully establishing industrial and agricultural schemes, in banking and land development.

Development of education went ahead by leaps and bounds under the colonial government. The two largest English-medium missionary schools in Sarawak, St Joseph's and St Thomas's, both in Kuching, followed by their counterparts for girls, St Teresa's and St Mary's, took the lead soon after the war ended to bring up their academic standards from Cambridge Junior Certificate to Senior School Certificate or Form V, and later introduced the Higher School Certificate. State schools and colleges giving good secondary education sprang up over Sarawak and teachers' training colleges in Kuching, Miri, and Sibu prepared teachers for English and Chinese medium schools. State, British, and foreign scholarships also enabled serving local civil servants to undergo training courses abroad while those with the right qualifications for entry into Universities and other higher institutions of learning were given scholarship awards to acquire tertiary education or take up professional skills. Realizing the importance of improving Chinese educational standards, the Chinese community, through their community associations and the Chinese General Chamber of Commerce in Kuching or its equivalents in other Divisional chief towns introduced, almost simultaneously with the English-medium schools, Senior Middle School courses. The school boards in Kuching were combined to form a single board and it was placed under the central control of the Chinese Chamber of Commerce. The Chinese schools in the rural areas and those in the other Divisions continued, however, to retain their individual school board system, though all tried to raise educational standards.

Since Charles Brooke's days the Sarawak Government had been giving small grants to English-medium missionary schools whilst running a few vernacular schools teaching the Malay language. Little if anything was done for the Chinese community schools.[6] Under colonial administration the school grant system was improved and after the introduction of the Grant Code Regulations in 1956 all English- and Chinese-medium primary schools under the management of public school boards became full-fledged State-aided schools, whilst their teaching and administrative staff became civil servants, a status which their counterparts in State schools already enjoyed. One salutary outcome of the raising of educational standards in Sarawak was the appearance in the post-war period of an increasing number of local newspapers, the vast majority in the Chinese language, but several were in English and Malay. Before the war there was only one English publication, the *Sarawak Gazette*, a fortnightly to monthly magazine published since 1870 as a semi-official organ and chronicle of the Brooke administration.[7] By 1941 several Chinese dailies had made their appearance in Kuching and Sibu. The pre-war Chinese newspapers were published chiefly to disseminate news about the Sino-Japanese war which had broken out in 1937 and to encourage the Chinese community to give relief aid to China. They also carried local news items. On the other hand, post-war newspapers, both English and Chinese, contain international as well as Sarawak news, and strive to improve literary standards by including local contributions. For record purposes a list of major pre-war and post-war (up to the early

1960s) newspapers and magazines,* published in Chinese and English, is given below:

PRE-WAR NEWSPAPERS

Year	Where Published	Name of Publication	Language Medium	Remarks
1870	Kuching	Sarawak Gazette	English	Fortnightly/ monthly demi-official organ of Brooke administration
1927	Kuching	Syn Min Daily (新民日報)	Chinese	Publication ceased in 1930
1930?	Kuching	Yueh Feng Weekly (越風週報)	Chinese	Publication ceased after a while
1930?	Kuching	Kuching Daily Bulletin (古晉新聞日刊)	Chinese	Publication ceased after a while
1937	Kuching	Sarawak Daily News (砂勝越日報)	Chinese	Publication interrupted by Japanese occupation
1939	Sibu	Sibu Daily News (詩巫新聞日刊)	Chinese	Both dailies were combined in 1940 to form the Overseas Chinese Daily News
1939	Sibu	Er Chiang Daily (鵝江日報)	Chinese	
1940	Sibu	Overseas Chinese Daily News (華僑日報)	Chinese	Publication ceased in 1941; resumed in 1945

*Except for *Sarawak Gazette* and *Sarawak Vanguard* (English edition), all other publications were or are under Chinese management.

POST-WAR NEWSPAPERS

Year	Where Published	Name of Publication	Language Medium	Remarks
1945	Kuching	Chinese Daily News (中華日報)	Chinese	First published in 1945; in publication
1945	Kuching	Chung Hua Kung Pao (中華公報)	Chinese	Proscribed by government in 1951
1946	Kuching	Sarawak Tribune	English	In publication. Oldest post-war daily published in English.
1946	Kuching	The Review (時事評論)	Chinese	Bi-weekly publication; ceased 1948
1952	Kuching	Sarawak Vanguard (前鋒日報)	Chinese	Ceased publication in 1974 as a result of litigation.
1953?	Kuching	Sarawak Vanguard	English	English edition continues with Bahasa Malaysia columns
1956	Kuching	Sin Wen Pao (新聞報)	Chinese	Proscribed by government in 1962
1948	Sibu	Ta Tong Daily News (大同日報)	Chinese	First published in 1948
1950	Sibu	Chiao Sheng Pao (僑聲報)	Chinese	Proscribed by government in 1952

POST-WAR NEWSPAPERS (*Continued*)

Year	Where Published	Name of Publication	Language Medium	Remarks
1952	Sibu	See Hwa Daily News (詩華日報)	Chinese	In publication; with a branch in Kuching
1956	Sibu	Syn Ming Pao (新民報)	Chinese	Proscribed by government in 1957
1960	Sibu	Ming Chung Pao (民衆報)	Chinese	Proscribed by government in 1962
1954	Miri	Miri Weekly (美里週報)	Chinese	Ceased publication after one month
1957	Miri	Miri Chinese Daily News (美里日報)	Chinese	In publication
1961	Miri	Sarawak Peoples' Daily (砂民時報)	Chinese	Proscribed by government in 1962

OTHER KUCHING PUBLICATIONS INCLUDING MAGAZINES

Min Chung Tao Pao (民衆導報), Chinese daily (1955–6)

Hua Chiao Evening News (華僑晚報), Chinese daily (1956–8)

Sarawak Times (砂勝越時報), Chinese daily (1958–62)

Sin Shen Magazine (心聲月刊), Chinese monthly magazine (1957); ceased after seven issues

Literary Life Magazine (文藝生活月刊), Chinese monthly magazine; ceased after five issues

Sa'ati (團結報), official organ of SUPP; published in English, Chinese and Bahasa Malaysia

In its efforts to accelerate the pace of self-government for Sarawak the colonial government introduced in 1948 the Local Authority Ordinance which gave the Governor power to set up District and Divisional Councils in all parts of Sarawak, and made provision for elected membership on these councils. Under the Ordinance members were to be elected, not appointed, to the District councils from which they were to be elected to Divisional Councils. The Divisional Councils served as electoral colleges for membership to Council Negri. The Local Authority Ordinance, 1948, therefore laid the foundation for the three-tier election system[8] which was to follow in the local council elections in 1959 and provide the basis for Sarawak's first general election in 1963. The establishment of mixed (i.e. all races) local councils under the Ordinance for the first time provided the opportunity for Chinese leaders who were not appointed *kapitans* or area headmen to participate in local government. But, at the same time, the Ordinance also offered a chance to those who were able to manoeuvre themselves into leadership positions by means fair or foul to gain access to the council hierarchy.

Political observers saw the adoption of the Local Authority Ordinance introducing elected membership on local councils not merely as a step towards preparing the indigenous peoples for a more democratic form of government, but rather as an attempt to re-organize traditional Chinese leadership and thus partly to satisfy the desire of many sections of the Chinese community who had expressed in no uncertain manner their disillusionment with their own leaders. However, the implementation of the Local Authority Ordinance did not achieve the desired effect. In spite of the formation of local councils and the election of councillors, the traditional appointments of *kapitans* and area headmen were still retained, and the social and economic power wielded by a select group of wealthy merchants and others as recognized leaders continued to ensure that the Chinese Chamber of Commerce[9] remained the primary political link between the government and the Chinese people. Moreover, the experiences of the war years, when the Chinese and other ethnic groups in Sarawak were at the mercy of the invaders, had changed irreversibly the attitude not only of the average Chinese towards Western authority and towards their own traditional leadership, but also that of the Chinese leaders themselves in their relations with the new Colonial administration. This was to be soon revealed in the rather strained relationship between them in the early days over the handling of matters affecting the Chinese community.

Meanwhile the simmering discontent felt before the war by young, educated Chinese towards the Sarawak Government's conservative socio-economic policies and with their own over-privileged leaders (aggravated by the discovery that many respected leaders were only too willing to collaborate with the Japanese) became an open struggle for leadership soon after the establishment of the colonial government. These young rebels, mostly imbued with leftist ideology and polarized towards China, spurred on by the ideological struggle taking place in China at the time, had infiltrated into various front organizations through which they built a power base. Their own men were placed in key positions from which they tried to oust or replace traditional leaders from urban and rural communal organizations, school boards and, after the Local Authority Ordinance came into force, the local councils. These young radicals were members of, or involved in, an underground communist organization named Clandestine Communist Organisation (CCO) by the government; it was also known as SCO or Sarawak Communist Organisation which was established at about this time. The CCO followed the strategy of the Malayan Communist Party and was rural-based though it had cells in all levels of society. Its objective was to make Sarawak into a communist state. It began by infiltrating into established organizations and institutions to gain control of their leadership and by fomenting and encouraging social unrest. It also recruited young members and prepared them for armed rebellion against the colonial government.

Four months after liberation twenty-two Chinese community associations combined to form the Chung Hua Association. This was intended to be a central body to express more representative views directly to the British Military Administration rather than through a multitude of dialect associations, and of bringing to the fore urgent problems of the Chinese community which had not been sufficiently emphasized by the Chinese Chamber of Commerce. The association's immediate objective was to clarify the Chinese position on the question of cession and its aim was the formation of a 'Chinese Democratic Political Society'. It also raised pressing issues including the resuscitation of Chinese education. These activities evidently did not meet with favour from the colonial government nor gain the support of the conservative Chamber. However, it had a short political life because its functions were soon assumed by the Chinese Advisory Board which the government set up in 1947, placing on it more conservative elements, and by the appointment of a Chinese consul in Kuching by the Nationalist Government at Nanking in 1948. Shortly after the consul's appointment, the Chinese Chamber of Commerce and the Chung Hua Association issued statements welcoming the new consul, adding that he would now become the representative of Sarawak Chinese to the Chinese government and to the local Sarawak government. This was a grave policy error. As Sarawak-born Chinese were regarded as British subjects they were not the responsibility of a foreign consul. The Sarawak government took immediate exception to the statements by complaining to both bodies as well as to the Chinese Consulate.

The change of regime from Nationalist to Communist on the Chinese mainland in 1949 ended official Kuomintang representation in Sarawak. It also emphasized the need for Sarawak Chinese to choose whether their loyalty lay with Sarawak or China. The government stressed that Britain's recognition of Communist China was not tantamount to any weakening of its resolve to oppose the extension of communism into the British territories.[10] Nevertheless, as a gesture of goodwill, the government granted permission to the Chinese community to celebrate the new Chinese National Day with mass meetings and rallies, while allowing the celebration of the Nationalist 'Double Tenth' to continue, although few Chinese associations sponsored it.

Two events occurred in the 1950s which caused great opposition from the Chinese community to the colonial government and acted as a catalyst for the subsequent formation of Chinese political parties. The first concerned Chinese education. As has been mentioned already, a system of Chinese school boards under the direction of the community associations and ultimately the control of the Chinese Chamber of Commerce was, and still is, responsible for the management of urban Chinese schools in Sarawak, while local school boards conducted the rural schools. Until the war most school board members came from among the traditional leaders and were therefore conservative in outlook. After the war radical young leaders began to challenge effectively the conservatives' control of the schools. After a series of incidents in the early 1950s they were able to take over, and the Chinese school system, as a whole, came to be the focus of new Chinese leadership opposed to the old. The Chinese schools thus became the scene of sporadic conflict as the government extended more rigid control over activities formerly within the Chinese education system, and sought to bolster up the authority of those who could halt the leftward trend. In 1951, leftist-inspired students in Kuching numbering some 200 went on strike. The school affected was closed, and the government's reaction was to bring criminal charges against the ring-leaders and to proscribe two youth organizations considered subversive. A Kuching Chinese newspaper with a leftist stand and widely read by students and workers was also proscribed in the same year. In early 1954, the government itself precipitated a confrontation by deleting from its register of accredited schools the 17th Mile (Kuching–Serian Road) Chinese school for alleged pro-communist activity by its teaching staff and board of management. The following year middle-school students in Kuching staged a two-month strike which was ended only after direct government intervention. Other incidents occurred in Kuching, Sibu, and Miri, exacerbated, in government's view, by the refusal or inability of school boards to take firm action against dissenters.

The precarious financial situation of Chinese school teachers, employed on the goodwill of school boards and dependent for their remuneration on the state of the schools' finances (which in turn were dependent on public generosity and on a form of levy upon merchants and others) made them particularly vulnerable to any concerted pressure from those opposed to their political views. The government, partly to remedy the worsening situation and partly to attempt, for the first time, to assist and redirect the Chinese school system, published in 1955 a White Paper containing new Grant Code Regulations, based upon the Woodhead Report, on financing education in Sarawak and on the terms and conditions of service in the teaching profession.[11] The grant code was to take effect from 1956. Woodhead, after a careful study, had made substantial recommendations for the Chinese schools. He noted their reliance on donations and suggested a bargain by which the government gave massive financial aid to the schools in return for government control over the curriculum. Interpreting his proposal as a government move to destroy or curb Chinese education, the Central School Board through the Chamber of Commerce rejected the Woodhead proposals out of hand, while a 'Preserve Chinese Education' committee was formed to solicit support from all over Sarawak. However, an *ad hoc* Sarawak Education Council, established as a result of a suggestion from Sarikei, where local Chinese representatives had not rejected the government proposals, was able after long discussion to resolve by thirteen votes to twelve to accept the new grant regulations.

The second event was the introduction of trade licensing fees. Council Negri approved in December 1954 a revised scale of fees designed to produce an additional revenue of $3.5 million per annum for providing the educational expansion envisaged in the Woodhead Report. The new rates amounting, in some cases, to increases of over 1,000 per cent, were to take effect from 1 January 1955. On Christmas Day the Sarikei Chinese Chamber of Commerce held a protest meeting and resolved to close all shops for the first ten days of the new year. Binatang shopkeepers followed suit, then Sibu and Kuching. The hartal (closure) soon spread to Bintulu, Miri, and throughout Sarawak.[12] Representatives from all major trading centres in Sarawak converged on Kuching to make their feelings known to government. In consequence of this unprecedented pressure, government postponed the application of the new fees, appointed a committee of inquiry with significant local representation to work out revised fees, and a modified Bill was presented to Council Negri two months later.

1. They were Ong Hap Leong, a son of Ong Tiang Swee, Tan Sum Guan, Kho Peng Loong, and Tze Shuen Sung.

2. This information can be found in Basil Collyer's book: *The War in the Far East 1941–1945* (London: Heinemann, 1969).

3. Those interested should read Robert Payne, *The White Rajahs of Sarawak* (London: Robert Hale Ltd., 1960) and a number of other histories of Sarawak written since the war. The same books also give detailed accounts of the cession controversy and of the anti-cession movement which climaxed in the assassination of the second Governor of Sarawak, Duncan Stewart, in Sibu in 1949.

4. See *Sarawak Gazette* of 2 September 1946 (also its first post-war issue). Both the *Gazette* and the official reports of Council Negri carry the full texts of members' speeches on the cession issue.

5. *Land Rules, 1933.*

6. An example was the Hokkien Free School, for a long time the largest Chinese community school. For this school Charles Brooke made available $4\frac{1}{2}$ acres of land at its present Tabuan Road site, in exchange for a strip of land at Wayang Street. He also presented four steel girders for the main building and supplied drawing plans for the school's construction.

7. The *Sarawak Gazette* remains in publication to this day. Publication ceased only during the Japanese occupation years. For many years now the *Gazette* has appeared in two separate editions: the *Sara-*

wak Government Gazette containing Sarawak's legislation, government regulations, notifications, etc., and the *Sarawak Gazette* which continues to carry articles of topical and general interest.

8. Under the system of indirect elections in Sarawak, a candidate had first to be elected to the District Council, and then the Divisional (Advisory) Council. From the Divisional Council, he would finally be elected to Council Negri. The District and Divisional Councils therefore acted as electoral colleges. Since the election procedure involved three levels it was popularly known as the three-tier system.

9. In 1978 a Pan-Malaysian Chinese General Chamber of Commerce was established. The Sarawak Chinese Chamber not only played a leading role in its formation but also provided its first President, Wee Boon Ping.

10. *Sarawak Tribune*, 7 January 1950.

11. E. W. Woodhead, *The Financing of Education and Conditions of Service in the Teaching Profession in Sarawak* (GPO, 1955).

12. *Sarawak By the Week*, a weekly publication of the Sarawak Information Service, No. 21 (24–30 May 1959).

9
Chinese in Party Politics

THE FORMATION OF PARTIES

THE negotiations between the Sarawak government and the Chinese representatives on the issues of education and commerce (dealt with in the preceding chapter) were political in character and brought to the fore a number of leaders from *ad hoc* bodies in Kuching, Sarikei, and elsewhere, men of talent and outstanding leadership. With them the idea was already gaining ground that the time had come, especially in view of the government's adoption of the election system in local councils,[1] for the formation of a political party, as a more permanent organization capable of safeguarding and promoting the democratic rights of the Chinese and other communities. These leaders soon combined to explore the depth of popular support for such a party; and those who had led the negotiations opposing the government's policy on Chinese education and trade licensing were naturally chosen to be the prime movers for the party's formation. Their experiences were coupled with heightened political activity both in Malaya and Singapore, and their expectations were encouraged by Sarawak's then Chief Secretary, J. H. Ellis, who was conscious of the need for the first Sarawak political party to be under the control of leaders who were friendly with the administration. He circulated an internal government memorandum to that effect and suggested that Ong Kee Hui should become its leader.[2]

Ong Kee Hui and Stephen Yong Kuet Tze,[3] a lawyer, who had played a key role the previous year in a special committee established to resolve the two-month student strike, began early in 1956, together with two other lawyer friends, to raise the subject of launching a multi-racial political party. Approaches were accordingly made to the Malay National Union and the Sarawak Dayak Association. Their response was poor and they indicated that each would, at the appropriate time, form a racial party of its own. Meanwhile private encouragement was given by the Governor, Sir Anthony Abell, to Ong Kee Hui to form a broadly representative non-racial party, but the principal difficulty was the absence of significant native interest and support. In 1959, encouraged by a local newspaper article written by an influential young Malay which introduced the possibility of real native participation, Ong Kee Hui and his friends set about founding the Sarawak United People's Party (SUPP), a party to be 'non-communal in character, with emphasis on loyalty to Sarawak and unity of all races'.[4] Native participation in the party, which had been hoped for, was after all not forthcoming, in spite of discreet efforts by the government and by Anthony Brooke. The latter was the central figure of the anti-cession movement in 1946, who wrote to the Malay National Union to encourage it to support the party formation. The Dayak leaders were either uninterested or non-committal.

A few weeks before the party's formal inauguration the Governor appeared to have changed his mind regarding government support. He cautioned that party politics essentially should not cause further divisions in Sarawak's multi-racial community but that it should be a unifying and binding force. If a party tended to be dominated by one race or class it might have the effect of disintegrating that community. He also expressed doubts whether at that stage of Sarawak's development political parties would spell faster progress for the country.[5] The government's ambivalent stand was allegedly caused by the knowledge that the Communist Clandestine Organisation was heavily infiltrating the SUPP ranks and its members were using the party as an open-front organization. The militant left-wing, usually young Chinese, did whole-heartedly support the SUPP. Their enthusiasm surprised the government and aroused native suspicion. Nevertheless party formation had gathered so much momentum that it could not be halted indefinitely; and so on 12 June 1959, the SUPP was officially inaugurated, thus beginning a new era in Sarawak politics.

· The SUPP has its headquarters in Kuching, but there are party branches and sub-branches throughout all the Divisions of Sarawak. Ultimate control is vested in a central committee of members who are elected by the delegates' conference. The day-to-day management of the party is handled by a smaller Central Working Committee. The SUPP leadership is mainly moderate in the top echelons while at the branch level the militant left is believed to have held sway. In spite of one major crisis in 1965 over the participation of SUPP in the Malaysian Solidarity Convention which caused a split between the moderates and the militants, resulting in the temporary resignation of the party Chairman and the Secretary-General, the moderates have remained in control. The party's member-ship is slanted in favour of the Chinese. There is, however, a good percentage of Dayak (Iban and Land Dayak) members. According to figures made available by the SUPP in 1963 the percentage of the ethnic composition of the party member-ship was as follows: Chinese 54 per cent, predominantly Hok-kiens and Hakkas; Ibans 32 per cent; Land Dayaks 6.5 per cent; the others were Malay, Melanau, and other indigenous groups.[6]

Another Chinese political party, the Sarawak Chinese As-sociation (SCA), made its appearance in July 1962. The SCA was led by wealthy Chinese who, with the imminent approach of independence for Sarawak through Malaysia, had perceived the need for an alternative political organization to SUPP. The SUPP had gained substantial support from the Chinese community, but the base of such support had come mainly from farmers, salaried workers, and other labouring classes. The party was therefore committed to remain socialist in outlook and might well be left completely outside the government. By mid-1962 moves were made, with the encouragement of the Malayan government, to establish an alliance of Sarawak right-wing parties, similar to that which had successfully governed the Malay Federation for the past few years. With the encouragement of the Malayan Chinese Association, the SCA pledged to work towards communal unity as a preliminary to broader national unity, to be achieved through an alliance of racial parties. The SCA also considered the possibility of affiliation with the MCA.[7]

The SCA was founded by men from two business groups, the Kuching Teochews and the Sibu Foochows. Its first president, William Tan, is a Teochew while his successor is a Foochow.[8] Both groups were conspicuously absent from the membership of the SUPP. The SCA included other founders, the younger English-educated Chinese and others dissatisfied with the predominantly Chinese-educated membership of the SUPP. It also attracted to its ranks the older, more conservative Chinese-educated who regarded the SUPP as a party of young upstarts and resented its activities; but the SCA was doomed from the beginning by its almost total failure to engender enthusiasm among the young. This is explained by its image as another Chinese association, an exclusive club for wealthy businessmen and others of the past era seeking to perpetuate their influence by participation in the new Malaysian ruling élite.

The SCA had a small but select membership believed to have been 2,000 to 3,000 at its peak. The Kuching group formed a majority of members of the first Central Committee. With the approach of Sarawak's first general election in 1963 feelings of dissatisfaction arose within the party over alleged inadequate funding and preparation for the SCA campaign. This resulted in changes in the composition of the Central Committee. William Tan was ousted from the presidency and made patron of the association, and Ling Beng Siew of Sibu took over as president. Later the party came under the control of the Third Division Foochows where more than half of the twenty-three Central Committee members lived. But the coalition government of Party Bumiputra and the Chinese SUPP (which had been in opposition) formed after the general election of 1970 greatly reduced the SCA's potential as a Chinese party. After the Sarawak Barisan Nasional (PBB-SUPP Coalition) won the 1974 elections the SCA decided to dissolve itself and some of its members joined the SUPP.

It is significant that whereas the SCA was always regarded by the Chinese public as a pro-government party sponsored by the rich and influential, the SUPP was, in spite of having 'blue bloods' in its leadership, usually considered to be a party covering all strata of Chinese society, especially the Chinese-educated who had no easy access to those in power. This was undoubtedly an induced reality brought about by its grass-roots Chinese membership of the common people, and the fact of its branch level organizations being infiltrated and/or controlled by leftist elements who in Sarawak, as elsewhere, always identify themselves with the masses. SUPP's opposition to Malaysia (explained not as conceptual objection but opposition to the manner in which the British government and Malaya had brought it about) and its increased gathering of native (Dayak) support in the rural areas hitherto receptive to all government's proposals, made it a *non grata* party to the colonial government, particularly at the time of Malaysia's formation. Following the Brunei revolt in 1962, the government introduced a series of emergency ordinances[9] containing specific regulations such as the Preservation of Public Security Regulations, 1962, to deal expressly with rebels and subversives. Under the emergency regulations any person suspected of involvement in subversive activities could be detained without trial up to a period of two years. Such preventive detention could not be challenged in a law court. A month after the passage of the Preservation of Public Security Bill four SUPP central committee members were detained and left the country on deportation orders.[10] Later more SUPP members at different levels and many others (CCOs and subversives) were arrested and detained or placed under restriction orders. Three radically left-wing Chinese language papers strategically located in Kuching, Sibu, and Miri were proscribed on government's orders. The effect was that SUPP did not do so well as the Sarawak Alliance (coalition of SNAP, PESAKA, BARJASA and SCA) at the first general election in 1963, and it became the opposition party. One other direct result of the implementation of the emergency ordinances was to drive underground a large number of SCOs in front organizations and send many of its young members across the border to Indonesian Borneo, where a legal and politically active communist party was in existence. There they received military training. When Sukarno launched his confrontation campaign against Sarawak for choosing to enter Malaysia early in 1963 the young Chinese communists returned in force with Indonesian 'volunteers' to begin their attacks on towns on Sarawak's borders.

Once party politics appeared in Sarawak the Chinese were eager to participate. Except for the civil servants and members of the armed forces who were in any case debarred from taking an active part in politics, large numbers of urban and rural Chinese of all dialect groups joined the SUPP, while a select number of Foochows and Teochews joined the SCA. A few also became members of other political parties, some with constitutions providing for multi-racial membership, which other racial groups had established. The first of these was Party Negara Sarawak (PANAS), founded in 1960 by the procession Malay leader, the late Datu Bandar Abang Haji Mustapha. PANAS' membership consisted mainly of Malays but it also included a number of Dayaks and some wealthy Chinese. Next came Party Ra'ayat Jati Sarawak (BARJASA), established in 1961 by Malay leaders who opposed cession, under the chairmanship of Datu Tuanku Haji Bujang, who later became the second Governor of Sarawak after the formation of Malaysia. BARJASA did allow a few Chinese to join it (one appeared on the central executive in 1962) but they were never in a position to influence policy. In 1967 the two Malay parties were merged into Party BUMIPUTRA. Also in 1961 the first Dayak party, the Sarawak National Party (SNAP) was formed under the chairmanship of Stephen Kalong Ningkan and other Ibans who had at one time or another worked with Shell Oilfields Ltd. in Brunei or in adjacent areas of Sarawak. SNAP at first confined its membership to Dayaks but changed its policy in 1964 to admit two Chinese into its eighteen-member Central Executive Committee. Another Dayak party, Pesaka Anak Sarawak (PESAKA), was registered in 1962 with Temenggong Jugah anak Barieng as its founder president. This party's membership is exclusively Dayak. Yet another political party was formed in 1964. Known as MACHINDA it was organized as an inter-racial party consisting of Malay, Chinese, and Dayak membership. The founding members consisted of those who were dissatisfied with PANAS because of its negotiations, together with BARJASA, with West Malaysia's UMNO for a direct linkup of Malay racial parties in Sarawak, and a few other politicians who had resigned from their own parties for one reason or another. There was unfortunately little common unity of aim and a marked absence of good leadership. Soon personal differences developed into conflict within the leadership ranks. Within two years of its formation both the chairman and the secretary of the party resigned and late in 1966 its second secretary led a group of members to join PESAKA. The party was formally dissolved in early 1967 and the remaining Land Dayak members joined SNAP.

CHINESE PARTICIPATION IN GOVERNMENT

The local authority elections held in 1959 to return elected councillors to each District Council offered ample opportunity for Chinese leaders at district level to contest for political leadership. Young Chinese leaders, in both urban and rural areas, duly took advantage of the chance. Many of them were members of the recently formed SUPP. With Malaysia soon to come into being the Sarawak government decided, early in 1963, to hold the first general election to Council Negri which, since its amended Constitution of 1957, had an enlarged elected membership. The election was held from April to June 1963, under the three-tier system. In accordance with the provision of the *Inter-Governmental Committee Report on Malaysia*,[11] the 1963 election was to be the last indirect election for Sarawak. A ministerial system, under British tutelage, was introduced after the election in order to prepare the newly-elected Ministers for a short period of internal self-government before Sarawak gained full independence as a member of the Federation of Malaysia. The latter came into being on 16 September 1963.

All political parties except SUPP and PANAS joined together to form the Sarawak Alliance to contest the 1963 election. Polling took place during April and May for the 429 seats on the District Councils and the voting results are given below:

Alliance	138	PANAS	59
SUPP	116	Independent	116

Subsequent elections at Divisional Council level resulted in the thirty-six unofficial seats of Council Negri being distributed as follows:

Alliance	19	PANAS	3
SUPP	5	Independent	9

Following the election the first ministerial government of Sarawak was formed, consisting of 6 Alliance members in the following ratio: SNAP 3; BARJASA 2; SCA 1. The expatriate State Secretary, Financial Secretary, and Attorney-General remained ex-officio members. Two Chinese Ministers were admitted to the cabinet: SCA's Teo Kui Seng and James Wong Kim Min, an independent who subsequently joined SNAP. Crises later occurred in the new cabinet. After the Alliance crisis of 1966[12] the Chief Minister, Stephen Kalong

Ningkan, was removed from office and Penghulu Tawi Sli was appointed Chief Minister in his place.

In 1969 Sarawak was ready to proceed with its first direct general election since joining Malaysia. Polling began throughout Malaysia on 10 May and in West Malaysia it was completed and the results announced the following day. In East Malaysia voting was staggered. Because of events in Kuala Lumpur on 13 May which led to communal rioting, the Federation government suspended the constitutional process and declared a state of national emergency throughout Malaysia. Consequently on 15 May polling was suspended in Sarawak.

The election was resumed in June 1970. The voting results were as follows:

Political Party	Number of Members Elected	Percentage of Total Votes Cast
SUPP	12	28.9
SNAP	12	24.5
BUMIPUTRA	12	14.7
PESAKA	8	13.7
SCA	3	10.7
Independent	1	7.6
	48	100

Much to the surprise of all who had come to identify SUPP with the opposition role, after the election SUPP and BUMIPUTRA formed a coalition government (with 24 seats) instead of the anticipated tripartite alliance of BUMIPUTRA-PESAKA-SCA (with 23 seats) or a likely coalition of SUPP and SNAP (with 24 seats).

The coalition cabinet of 1970 consisted of 6 Ministers, 1 Malay, 1 Melanau (in the person of the Chief Minister, Datuk Patinggi Haji Abdul Rahman Yaakub), 2 Dayaks (Ibans) and 2 Chinese. The 2 Chinese Ministers were Stephen Yong (SUPP) who was made a Deputy Chief Minister and Minister for Communications and Works, and Sim Kheng Hong (SUPP), Minister for Local Government. Unfortunately Ong Kee Hui, Chairman of SUPP, was unsuccessful in his contest of the Kuching Barat constituency, but he was returned in the Parliamentary constituency of Bandar Kuching. In due course he was made a Federal Minister.

The militant Sarawak Communist Organization (SCO) which had been urging unsuccessfully a total boycott of the 1970 general election became even more hostile and stepped up a terrorist campaign soon after the formation of the coalition government. The significance of the communist timing appears to be that the communist organization in Sarawak now found it could no longer pursue an open-front strategy through SUPP, and that communist supporters no longer saw SUPP as a credible vehicle. When SUPP leaders were in the opposition they faced a situation where their whole party was regarded as crypto-communist. Now its role had been reversed to pro-government, as even the party's Secretary-General and Deputy Chief Minister had become an important member of the Security Committee. The rank and file therefore directed mounting dissatisfaction and much criticism at their leaders, in particular Ong Kee Hui, for accepting a Federal ministership. The members felt that their leaders, by joining forces with the government and having to follow government policies, were in fact reneging on their promise to secure the release or trial in the law courts of those detained under the Preservation of Public Security Regulations. They considered that their leaders were now in an even worse position to negotiate with the Federal government on behalf of the detainees who were in any case willing to accept only an unconditional release.

However, it is fair to say that the Chinese public on the whole were happy with SUPP's role in government. The party's coalition with BUMIPUTRA has provided stability in Sarawak politics and thus enabled the country to proceed with its economic and social development plans. It has also allowed a party with definite objectives to play its part in implementing government policies in economic development and expansion, and in sensitive areas concerning education and national language calculated to benefit people of all races, while it has not neglected the constitutional and traditional rights of the Chinese. Not least was SUPP's contribution towards efforts which enabled the Chief Minister, Datuk Patinggi Haji Abdul Rahman Yaakub, to negotiate with the top leaders of the Sarawak Communist Organization for a peace settlement known as the Sri Aman agreement, concluded in March 1974. This agreement brought to an end active communist armed struggle and enabled hundreds of communist terrorists in the jungles to return to normal society, thus reducing communist insurgency to minimal proportions.

With the communist terrorist threat all but removed the Sarawak coalition government decided to call for the second direct general election which had been postponed for security reasons. (Elections were held in West Malaysia in 1973.) The name of the coalition government had meanwhile been changed to the Sarawak National Front (Barisan Nasional Sarawak). There was also a slight change in the alignment of the party BUMIPUTRA. It became Parti Bumiputra Bersatu as a result of a new merger between it and PESAKA. Barisan Nasional (BN) was the brain-child of the late Tun Abdul Razak, the second Prime Minister of Malaysia. Under BN all political parties forming part of the ruling government of Malaysia were grouped into one national party alliance.

The 1974 election took place between August and September, and in East Malaysia it was staggered because the electorate is scattered over far-flung areas. In this election SNAP found itself in the new role of opposition party. But it was a strong and well-united opposition which fielded, no less than the Sarawak BN, candidates with professional and academic qualifications to contest both the State and Parliamentary constituencies. The election resulted in unexpected surprises. SNAP won 18 out of the 48 Council Negri (State) seats and 9 out of the 24 Parliamentary seats; 3 out of its 18 State and 1 out of its 9 Parliamentary seats were gained by its Chinese candidates. The party's Vice-Chairman, James Wong, was returned in his Limbang state constituency although defeated in the parliamentary constituency of Miri-Subis. The most spectacular win was scored by Lo Foot Kee who defeated SUPP's Stephen Yong in the Kuching Timur state constituency, though Stephen Yong won in his Parliamentary constituency of Padawan. As a component of Barisan Nasional, SUPP performed well during the elections. Its candidates gained 9 out of 12 State seats and 5 out of 7 Parliamentary seats in a total of 30 State and 15 Parliamentary seats won by the PBB-SUPP alliance. The Chief Minister subsequently enlarged his coalition cabinet from 7 to 13 members, 3 of whom were Assistant Ministers. Sim Kheng Hong was made Deputy Chief Minister in place of Stephen Yong and also held the Land and later Finance and Development portfolio. Dr Wong Soon Khai, a new Minister, was made Minister for Agriculture and Community Development. Ong Kee Hui who retained his Parliamentary seat of Kuching Bandar, continued as a Federal Minister.

A historic event which affected the balance of Chinese participation in State government occurred in 1976 when SNAP entered the Sarawak Barisan Nasional, thus relinquishing its opposition role. SNAP's entry into the Barisan Nasional resulted from protracted negotiations between the Chief Minister and his BN colleagues and the SNAP leadership, which ended in the party being officially accepted as a component of Barisan Nasional on 20 June 1976, at the same time as Sabah's newly-emerged Parti Berjaya and the defeated USNO (which had been specially allowed to remain as a pro-government party) were admitted into Barisan Nasional. The resultant reshuffling of his cabinet enabled the Chief Minister to include Ministers from SNAP ranks, and also brought about the appointment of two Chinese Assistant Ministers, Lo Foot Kee of SNAP to the Ministry of Local Government and Chong Kiun Kong of SUPP to the Ministry of Communications and Works. Both were sworn in on 1 November 1976.

On 8 June 1978, Datuk Hussein Onn, the Prime Minister of Malaysia, announced general elections once more for State and Parliamentary constituencies. Parliament was dissolved on 12 June and nomination day was 21 June. Polling began from 8 July, but as it was staggered in East Malaysia it was concluded only on 22 June.

In West Malaysia both State and Parliamentary elections were held simultaneously in all states except Kelantan where an emergency State election had been held earlier in the year. In the two East Malaysian states of Sabah and Sarawak, only Parliamentary elections were held as Sabah's last State elections did not take place till 1976 and Sarawak's would not be due till 1979. Both Legislative assemblies of these States had decided to serve their full five-year terms.

In Sarawak the 1978 Parliamentary elections were presaged by the formation of several new political parties, Parti Rakyat Jati Sarawak (PAJAR), Sarawak People's Organization (SAPO) based in Miri, Parti Negara Rakyat Sarawak (PNRS or PEACE), United Malaysia Timur Organization (UMAT), and Parti Berasa. In addition there were many independents, some of whom were former members of established parties. Two of these had been SUPP members who were also members of Council Negri. Their departure from the party reduced SUPP's State seats from 12 to 10. All the new political parties (except BERJASA) contested the elections as opposition parties to Sarawak Barisan Nasional. The largest of them, PAJAR, was led by Alli Kawi, a former senior police officer and a lawyer, and it fielded thirteen candidates.

The support for Barisan Nasional was overwhelming both in West and East Malaysia. This support enabled BN to win 94 out of the 114 Parliamentary seats (a few uncontested) and 241 out of the 276 State seats in the eleven states of West Malaysia. The remaining seats went to the Democratic Action Party (DAP): 15 Parliamentary and 24 State seats, and independents 2 State seats. In Sabah, Barisan Nasional gained 14 out of the 16 Parliamentary seats while the remaining 2 seats went to DAP and an independent. Barisan Nasional Sarawak had a sweeping victory. Its candidates won all but 1 of the 24 Parliamentary seats. This victory increased BN's seats in Parliament to a record 131 out of a total of 154 seats. Barisan Nasional Sarawak's only defeat occurred in the Lambir (formerly Miri-Subis) constituency where its candidate, SUPP's Chia Chin Shin, was defeated by a young lawyer, Raymond Szetu Mei Thong, Secretary-General of the recently formed SAPO and the sole candidate from his party to contest. PAJAR unexpectedly suffered complete defeat, with not even a single seat being won by its thirteen candidates. The defeat of Chia Chin Shin thus left SUPP with 6 of its 7 candidates retaining their Parliamentary seats, of which 5 were won by Chinese candidates (including Stephen Yong's Padawan seat which was retained uncontested).

Datuk Hussein Onn formed his new 'people inspired' Malaysian cabinet on 28 July, a week after the close of the elections. Although he appointed two new Ministers to this cabinet from Sarawak Barisan Nasional, the position of its only Chinese Minister in this cabinet remained unchanged. SUPP's Ong Kee Hui, having once again been returned with an overwhelming majority in the Bandar Kuching Parliamentary constituency, was reinstated in his old portfolio of Minister of Science, Technology, and Environment.

In January 1979 SNAP's Assistant Minister for Local Government, Lo Foot Kee, passed away suddenly. In the by-election that followed in March in his former constituency of Kuching Timur (now Padungan), the BN-sponsored Chinese candidate (SNAP), Chai Chong Fea, was surprisingly defeated by an Independent, Dr Chua Kok Beng, by a landslide majority of 5,737 votes.

After the 1978 Parliamentary election one of the 13 Sarawak State Ministers became a Federal Minister, thus leaving the State Barisan Nasional cabinet with 12 members, 8 of whom were full Ministers (the list included 1 Chief Minister, 3 Deputy Chief Ministers, 4 Ministers holding portfolios and 4 Assistant Ministers). Lo Foot Kee's death temporarily reduced the number by one. This eleven-member cabinet consisted of 3 Malays (one a woman), 3 Ibans, 3 Chinese, 1 Melanau and 1 Kayan. The composition well reflects the multi-racial nature of Sarawak's population and the plurality of its society.

A state election for Sarawak was held in September 1979. Polling was staggered from September 15 to 22, and the full results were announced the following day. Barisan Nasional won an overwhelming victory, gaining 45 out of the 48 seats of Dewan Undangan Negri (Council Negri). The three remaining seats were gained by Independents. None of the opposition parties taking part, PAJAR, DAP, SAPO and UMAT, succeeeded in winning any seat. By its victory, BN not only retained all the seats (except one) of its members in Council Negri, but also increased its total seats in the Council when Stephen Yong regained his seat by winning in the Bengoh constituency, and when new members of BN defeated their opponents in other constituencies. As a result of the 1979 election 12 seats in Council Negri are now held by Chinese (11 are BN members and 1 is an Independent).

The new State Cabinet was sworn in on 26 September 1979, with a line-up of 7 full Ministers (including the Chief Minister) and 5 Assistant Ministers.[13] This ministerial line-up is substantially the same as before the election. In it the number of Chinese Ministers remains three: 2 full Ministers and 1 Assistant Minister.

CONCLUSION

The history of Sarawak's Chinese is progressive history. It is vibrant with life and growth. Not merely has it a credible past and a unique present, but more important it has also a great future, the quality of which can only be determined by the efforts of the present generation, working in harmony with people of other races. But the historian's function is essentially to record the facts of the past and the present. His role is neither to forecast the future nor to put forward his own views on how that future should be shaped. The latter is the work of our leaders if they have the interests of the country at heart. Whilst this is so, it is nevertheless incumbent on us, as ordinary citizens of Malaysia, without regard to differences of race, creed, or political leanings, to bring about a just and prosperous society for all, in Sarawak's context within the greater context of Malaysia. If historians consider it fitting to make critical observations let them do so honestly and without prejudice, within the limits of propriety and reasonableness.

In the past, lack of proper understanding of the Chinese way of life, their cultural differences and social background led successive administrations in Sarawak to think of them as aliens and to regard their intentions and motives with mistrust. Harsh criticisms had therefore been levelled at them for their money-making propensity, their exploitation of the economically backward, their inordinate attachment to their own culture, and their polarization towards China. But the major charge was that they had divided loyalties and that they resisted efforts at integration. The unfortunate presence of a group of militant communist terrorists who carried on a campaign of subversion and terrorism in the country lent much credence to this charge.

But with the emergence of Malaysia and its assiduous practice of parliamentary democracy, greater understanding between the different ethnic groups comprising Malaysia's multiracial population is now possible, given the goodwill and sincerity of all concerned. The sharing of political power, in Sarawak as in the rest of Malaysia, no less than the guarantee of basic freedoms to all races under the Malaysian Constitution, has come to be realized by the Chinese as evidence of the recognition of their rights as citizens, and provided them with a strong incentive to look upon Malaysia alone as their country, to whose fortunes they, together with other races, are inextricably bound. Announcements made recently by the People's Republic of China have helped to clarify the status of Overseas Chinese (that is Chinese born or having acquired citizenship in an overseas country, *vis-à-vis* China-born Chinese who retain their Chinese nationality). This shows that China has relinquished citizenship rights or control over those Chinese of the first two categories. The Chinese government also exhorts all Chinese nationals living abroad to obey the laws of their country of residence; this has removed all doubts and ambiguities. Overseas Chinese should realize where their true destiny now lies.

Under the protective umbrella of a multi-racial democratic system of government at Federal and State levels the Chinese in Sarawak can look forward to greater prosperity and progress, culminating in the attainment of long-term development goals which will increase the country's economic potentials and raise the living standards of all races, not least the Chinese.

But to achieve these goals calls for resolute efforts from the Chinese as well as other racial groups to work more closely together to remove any vestige of suspicion and fear of one race dominating another whether in the economic, social, or political field. This should be easier to accomplish in Sarawak where for many generations past there has been a strong tradition of harmonious relations and mutual respect between members of various races. It calls for better understanding and appreciation, for those in authority, of the nature and depth of some of the problems—economic, social, cultural, or educational—that still beset the Chinese community, and the urgent need for a positive approach to find suitable and lasting solutions which are not in conflict with national goals and ideals. Above all, it calls for closer unity within the Chinese community itself and the readiness to take any action that will further the cause of national unity. This can begin with determined attempts to break down social barriers that have for long impeded progress and kept apart people belonging to different dialect or clan groups, religious beliefs, and educational backgrounds.

In the interests of national goals Sarawak's Chinese leadership, both political and communal, must hold itself in readiness to sink personal differences, give up ambitions of personal aggrandizement, and subjugate sectional interests to the overall interests of the country and the nation. As leaders of their own people they are expected to be honest and constant in their endeavours to look after the needs of all people, individually and collectively, wherever such needs arise. The results of the last Parliamentary elections and recent state elections have given clear indications of the growing maturity of Sarawak's voters, Chinese and non-Chinese. The judicious exercise of their prerogative has left no room for doubt that the days of political opportunism are over and that support will only stay with a leadership prepared to live up to the expectations of their discerning electorate.

1. The first local authority to hold elections under the provisions of the Local Authority Ordinance, 1948, was the Kuching Municipal Council in 1956. By the end of 1959 most of the other local councils had held elections. Even the appointment of *kapitans* and native chiefs, traditionally by direct appointment, was changed in the post-war period to one of election by the people.

2. Ong Kee Hui is the grandson of Ong Tiang Swee, the illustrious Chinese leader mentioned in these pages. Educated in Kuching (St Thomas's School) and Singapore and a graduate of Serdang College of Agriculture in Malaya, he worked with the Agricultural Department, Sarawak, from 1936 to 1946 and then left the service to become the manager of Bian Chiang Bank founded by his father-in-law, Wee Kheng Chiang. At the time of the proposal to form a political party Ong was already a prominent Chinese leader in his own right, having become a member of the Kuching Municipal Council (he was its president from 1960 to 1965) which he represented in Council Negri. He was also English Secretary of the Kuching Chinese Chamber of Commerce.

3. Stephen Yong is a T'aipu (T'appu) Hakka. He studied in Chinese (T'ai Tung) and English (St Thomas's) schools in Kuching. After the war he became a merchant and in 1950 left for England to study law at Nottingham University. He qualified and returned to Sarawak to practise law with T. G. Dunbar. Later he set up his own practice.

4. *Sarawak Tribune*, 5 March 1959.

5. *Sarawak By the Week*, No. 21 (24–30 May 1959), Sarawak Information Service bulletin.

6. See Michael B. Leigh, *The Rising Moon*, Sydney University Press, 1974, p. 16.

7. *Sarawak Tribune*, 27 June 1962 and also 3 August 1962.

8. William Tan is the son of Tan Boh Seng, a pioneer Teochew leader appointed *kangchew* of Semengok area (7th Mile, Penrissen Road) during Charles Brooke's rule. Tan was educated at St Joseph's School.

He left the PWD in the early 1930s to travel round the world, the first Sarawakian Chinese to have done so, and to study architecture. On his return he went into the road and building contract business. He became a founder Vice-president of the Party Negara Sarawak founded by his old friend and schoolmate, the late Datu Bandar Abang Haji Mustapha. He was president of the first fully-elected Kuching Municipal Council (1956–9) and member of the Supreme Council from 1957 to 1959. He became the second Speaker of Council Negri after Malaysia. Ling Beng Siew, his Foochow successor, is an extraordinarily astute businessman, who has, by his own acumen and industry, built up from scratch a business that rivals any in Sarawak. He has been conspicuously successful in the timber industry.

9. The ordinances included the Restricted Residence Ordinance (1961), the Public Order Ordinance (1962), the Preservation of Security Ordinance (1962), the Societies (Amendment) Ordinance, the Trade Unions (Amendment) Ordinance, and the Local Newspapers Ordinance.

10. *Sarawak Tribune*, 4 July 1962.

11. Sarawak Council Negri, *Malaysia, Report of the Inter-Governmental Committee*, 1962 (SGPO 1963).

12. See Michael Leigh, *The Rising Moon*, Chapter 3, The Development of Politics, 1963–66.

13. 'Sarawak's State Constitution provides that the Supreme Council (Cabinet) shall consist of not more than 9 members (Ministers), including the Chief Minister, and not less than 5. It also provides for the appointment of not more than 8 Assistant Ministers.' *Sarawak Tribune*, 25 September 1979.

Appendix I

Memo of Agreement was made in duplicate between the Sarawak Government, on the first part, and Messrs. Nai Siong and Tek Chiong of Chop Sim Hock Chew Kang, hereinafter mentioned as the Contractors on the other part.

1. The Contractors agree to introduce into the Rejang River 1,000 adult Chinese agriculturalists, men, women, and about 300 children and to establish them in that river for the purpose of cultivating rice, vegetables, fruits, etc., but of these immigrants not more than one half are to be introduced during the first year, that is to say before June 30, 1911, and the rest the contractors undertake to introduce during the following year, that is to say between June 30, 1901 and June 30, 1902.

2. The Government undertakes to advance the Contractors the sum of $30 for each adult and $10 for each child so introduced, and of these advances two thirds shall be paid to

*As contained in the Rajah's Agreement Book, April 1893–December 1902. The original thirty-one articles had probably been incorporated into the seventeen paragraphs of the final agreement.

the Contractors in Singapore, and the balance at Kuching on the arrival of the immigrants there, and the Contractors undertake that the moiety of the immigrants to be introduced during the first year as mentioned in Paragraph I, shall be brought to their destination in the Rejang within 4 calendar months from the date they receive the advances in Singapore as above mentioned.

3. The Contractors undertake to repay all such advances to the Government within 6 years from the date of this Agreement as follows: Nothing to be paid by the Contractors during the first year; during each of the subsequent years one-fifth of the advances to be paid each year, that is to say $6, for each adult and $2 for each child in respect to the advances paid on their account in accordance with Section 2.

4. The Government undertakes to provide for the passages of the aforementioned immigrants from Singapore to the Rejang, or, in the event of the Contractors bringing these immigrants direct from China to the Rejang, the Government will pay the Contractors $5 for each immigrant as passage money.

5. The Government undertakes to provide the Contractors free of all rent or other charges for the term of 20 years from the date of this Agreement, sufficient land in the Rejang in the vicinity of Ensurai and Seduan streams, or elsewhere, for the proper settlement of the aforementioned immigrants and to insure that the immigrants shall get sufficient land for their purpose, the quantity of land being not less than 3 acres for each adult.

6. On the expiration of the above-mentioned term of 20 years any immigrant shall on his application be given a grant for the land occupied by him subject to Quit rent at the rate of 10 cents per acre per annum, provided that such land be fully cultivated.

7. In the event of the Government wishing to occupy any land taken up by any of the immigrants a fair sum shall be paid to such immigrants by the Government for disturbance in respect to crops, houses, etc.

8. The Government undertakes to make suitable landing places, roads, and paths.

9. On the recommendation of the Contractors the Government will recognize the appointment of any competent and suitable man as *kangchew* or headman of each village or settlement. The powers of such *kangchews* will be limited to the settlement of trivial disputes, boundary disputes, and other minor matters, but these powers will be more clearly defined by the Government when necessity subsequently arises for their appointments.

10. The Government guarantees full protection to immigrants from interference by Natives.

11. The Government will place no restrictions on the immigrants with respect to their planting or the scale of their produce, and they will be at liberty to plant what they please and sell where they like, but it is understood by the Contractors that the primary object in introducing these immigrants is the cultivation of rice, and they, on their part, undertake to see that this is not lost sight of.

12. The Government undertakes to ship all provisions, stores, etc. for the immigrants and produce sent by them to Kuching, on Government vessels at moderate rates of freight as opportunities of shipping by Government vessels afford, but the Government does not undertake to run steamers especially for the purpose of carrying such goods and produce but will do its best to assist the immigrants in this respect.

13. The Government will not permit any persons to visit the immigrants for the purpose of inducing them to gamble or to gamble with them, nor to sell opium to them. Gambling amongst the immigrants may be allowed, or not as decided to be advisable by the Government and the Contractors, and, if at any time it is allowed, it will be confined solely to immigrants under the supervision of their headmen, and such headmen will alone have the right to sell opium to the immigrants under their charge. The Government will make special arrangements with the Farmers from time to time to insure those rules being carried out effectually.

14. The Government will permit that a limited but sufficient number of muskets may be kept by the immigrants to protect their crops from the ravages of wild pigs, etc.

15. After the expiration of 2 years from the date of this Agreement should the immigrants be successful and their settlements be in a thriving condition the Government will permit others joining them from China, and will assist such fresh immigrants in as far as it may lay in its power to do so.

16. Should the Contractors be successful in carrying out the objects in respect to these immigrants and succeed in establishing prosperous settlement or settlements they will be permitted to conduct such trading operations as they may wish, and successful planters will be permitted to trade.

17. On their sureties for the repayment of the advances as agreed upon and mentioned in Paragraph 3 of the Contractors' offer:

Signed—Khoo Siok Wan, Lim Boon Kheng
and the said Khoo Siok Wan and Lim Boon Kheng do hereby affix their seals and sign their names as having duly given security for the Contractors in this respect.

Signed, sealed and delivered on the 9th day of July, 1900. (Signatures are Khoo, Lim, Wong Nai Siong and Tek Chiong, Contractors: Charles Brooke and C. A. Bampfylde, Government: George Muir of Paterson, Simons & Co., Witness; at Kuching, July 27, 1900.)

Appendix II

To Messrs. Chiang Cho Shiong and Tan Kung Shook,

With respect to your proposal to form a Company with the object of introducing Chinese immigrants into the Rejang River for the purpose of cultivating under the style of "Sok Jong Kong," I am prepared to grant you permission to do this under the following conditions:

1. The Government will reserve for the purpose of your project sufficient land at Sungei Lanang and its neighbourhood for the sole use of immigrants imported by your Company, for which no rental or other charges will be made, but no permanent grant will be given for this land, which will revert to Government when abandoned or no longer occupied, though so long as such land is cultivated in a bona fide manner it will remain the property of your Company, and will not be subject to sale or transfer to others.

2. Such land may not be alienated in any way by your Company, nor made liable to any charges or payments.

3. The Government reserves the right of making roads and railways through any part of the above-mentioned reserve and of working minerals in the same but pay just compensation for any damages and disturbance where such roads and

railways pass through or such minerals are worked on cultivated land.

4. *A kangchew* may be appointed by your Company to keep order amongst the immigrants and settle all small disputes, reporting to the Resident of the District all crimes and offence(sic); the appointment of the *kangchew* will be subject to the approval of the Government. Police assistance will be provided when necessary and the immigrants will receive full protection in every way.

5. All landing places, roads, paths and bridges will be made by the Government as required.

6. The Government will supply the Company with a site at Sibu for the purpose of building stores or godowns for keeping and storing provisions and produce belonging to the immigrants.

7. The Government undertakes to pay the Company $5 for every adult immigrant introduced by them into the Rejang the number of whom, however, is to be limited to 5000, and no more than 500 adults (exclusive of children) are to be imported in any one year.

8. The Company will have the same right as others to fish in the rivers or the sea.

9. Arrangements will be made by the Government with the Government Farmers so that all farms may be held by the *kangchew* under the same terms as granted to *kangchews* in Gambier and Pepper districts. The exclusive rights so granted to the *kangchew* will extend only over the Reserve of land occupied by the immigrants and no other will be permitted to sell opium, spirits, arrack and wine or gamble with immigrants within that Reserve.

10. The immigrants may manufacture rice arrack to be used by their women when being confined, as is the case in China, but such arrack is to be made in small quantities only and on no account is to be sold.

11. The *kangchew* will have the sole right to sell stores and provisions required by the immigrants and to buy all produce obtained by them but strictly at local current market

rates. No others will be allowed to sell, buy or barter with the immigrants.

12. The Government will permit the Company to import firearms and ammunition for the use of the immigrants to protect their crops against wild pigs and other animals, but permits must first be obtained to import such firearms and ammunition.

13. The Government will grant to the Company under permanent lease a piece of land to be used solely as a burial ground.

14. The Government will assist the Company as far as possible in carrying on Government steamers at the usual rate of freights all stores, provisions and produce belonging to the Company or the immigrants.

15. In the event of the Company failing to establish a colony of not less than 500 adults on the Reserve of land mentioned above within one year from this date the conditions mentioned herein will be terminated.

Given under my hand and seal at Kuching, Sarawak, this 5th day of March, 1901.

Charles Brooke, Rajah

Bibliography

BOOKS

Avray, Harry, *Triad 21* (New English Library, Times Mirror, 1977).

Baring-Gould, S., and Bampfylde, C. A., *A History of Sarawak under its two White Rajahs, 1839–1908* (London: Henry Sotheran & Co., 1909).

Brooke, Charles Johnson, *Ten Years in Sarawak*, 2 vols. (London: 1866).

Bunyon, Charles John, *Memoirs of Bishop Francis Thomas McDougall and of Harriette His Wife* (London: 1889).

Chater, W. J., *Sarawak Long Ago* (Kuching: Borneo Literature Bureau, 1969).

Collyer, Basil, *The War in the Far East 1941–1945* (London: Heinemann, 1969).

Cooper, A. M., *Men of Sarawak* (Kuala Lumpur: Oxford University Press, 1968).

Dance, C. H., and Dartford, G. P., *Malayan and World History, Book I, Malaya and the World* (Longmans of Malaya, 1963).

De Groot, *Het Kongsiwezen van Borneo* (as quoted by Lo Hsiang-lin).

Earl, G. W., *The Eastern Seas* (London: 1837).

Gittings, J., *A Chinese View of China* (BBC London: 1973).

Hall, D. G. E., *A History of South-East Asia* (London: Oxford

University Press, 1965).

Harrisson, T. (ed.), *The Peoples of Sarawak* (Sarawak Government Printing Office, 1959).

_____, and O'Connor, Stanley J., *Excavations of the Prehistoric Iron Industry in West Borneo*, Vol. I, Data Paper No. 72, South-East Asia Program, Cornell University (New York, 1969).

Helms, Ludvig, *Pioneering in the Far East* (London: 1882).

Hose, Charles, and McDougall, William, *The Pagan Tribes of Borneo*, Vol. I (London: Frank Cass & Co., 1966).

Hunt, J., *Sketch of Borneo or Pulo Kalamantan, Communicated by J. Hunt, Esq., in 1812 to the Hon. Sir T. S. Raffles.*

Keppel, Henry, *A Visit to the Indian Archipelago in H.M.S. Meander* (London: 1853).

Leigh, Michael B., *The Rising Moon: Political Change in Sarawak* (Sydney University Press, 1974).

Li, Dun J., *Ageless Chinese* (London: J. M. Dent & Sons).

Liu Tze-chen, *Memories of Devastated Sibu* (See Hua Daily News Press, Sibu, 1955, 劉子政著：詩巫刼後追記).

Lo Hsiang-lin: *A Historical Survey of the Lan-fang Presidential System in Western Borneo, established by Lo Fang-pai and other Overseas Chinese* (羅香林著：西婆羅洲羅芳伯等所建共和國考) (Hong Kong: Institute of Chinese Culture, 1st ed. 1961).

Low, Hugh, *Sarawak* (London: 1848).

Outram, J. R., 'Sarawak Chinese', Tom Harrisson (ed.), *The Peoples of Sarawak* (SGPO, 1959).

Payne, Robert, *The White Rajahs of Sarawak* (London: Robert Hale, Ltd., 1960).

Pollard, Elizabeth, *Kuching, Past and Present* (Kuching: Borneo Literature Bureau, 1972).

Pringle, Robert, *Rajahs and Rebels* (London: Macmillan, 1970).

Purcell, Victor, *The Chinese in South-East Asia* (London: Oxford University Press, 1965). Also *Malaysia* (London: Thomas and Hudson, 1965).

Rawlins, Joan, *Sarawak, 1839–1968* (London: Macmillan & Co., 1969).

Runciman, Steven, *The White Rajahs* (Cambridge University Press, 1960).

Song Ong Siang, *One Hundred Years' History of Chinese in Singapore* (Reprinted by University of Malaya Press, Singapore, 1967).

St. John, H., *The Indian Archipelago, Its History and Present State*, vol. I (London: 1853).

St. John, Spenser, *Life in the Forests of the Far East* (London: 1863).

Templer, J. C., *The Private Letters of Sir James Brooke* (Edinburgh and London: William Blackwood & Sons, 1879).

T'ien Ju-kang, *The Chinese of Sarawak: A Study of Social Structure*, Monograph on Social Anthropology, No. 12 (London School of Economics and Political Sciences, 1953).

Willetts, William, *Chinese Art*, 2 vols. (London: Pelican Books (No. A 358), 1958).

Woodhead, E. W., *The Financing of Education and Conditions of Service in the Teaching Profession in Sarawak* (SGPO, 1955).

GOVERNMENT PUBLICATIONS

Laws of Sarawak, 1927–1935 (Red Book).

Malaysia: Report of the Inter-Governmental Committee, 1962.

Sarawak Gazette.

Sarawak Government Annual Report, 1962.

Sarawak Government Gazette.

Woodhead Report, *The Financing of Education and Conditions of Service in the Teaching Profession in Sarawak, 1955* (SGPO, 1955).

JOURNALS, MAGAZINES AND NEWSPAPER
ARTICLES

Braddell, R., 'An Introduction to the Study of Ancient Times in the Malay Peninsula and the Straits of Malacca', *Journal of the Royal Asiatic Society, Malayan Branch*, Vol. XIX, pt. 1., 1941.

Harrisson, T. and O'Connor, Stanley J., 'Gold in West Borneo', *Sarawak Museum Journal*, Vol. XVII, Nos. 34–35, July–December 1969.

Hipkins, James R., 'The History of the Chinese in Borneo', *Sarawak Museum Journal*, Vol. XIX, Nos. 38–39, July–December 1971.

Lockard, Craig A., 'Charles Brooke and the Foundations of the Modern Chinese Community in Sarawak, 1863–1917', *Sarawak Museum Journal*, Vol. XIX, Nos. 38–39, July–December 1971.

———, 'Leadership and Power within the Chinese Community of Sarawak: an Historical Survey', *Journal of South-East Asia Studies,* 11/2 (September 1971).

Logan J., 'Antiquity of Chinese Trade', *Journal of the Indian Archipelago and Eastern Asia*, Vol. II, No. IX, 1848.

Pringle, Robert, 'The Brookes of Sarawak: Reformers in Spite of Themselves', *Sarawak Museum Journal*, Vol. XIX, Nos. 38–39, July–December 1971.

T'ien Nung, *The Clan System in the Organisational Structure of Sarawak Chinese Community* (田農作：砂勝越華族社會結構中的幫派主義) published in the *Chinese Daily News* in its New Year's Day special edition of 1976. Also by the same: *Early Sarawak Chinese Leadership Hierarchy, 1841–1910* (田農作：砂勝越早期華族社會的領導層), *Chinese Daily News*, New Year's Day edition, 1977.

Wang Yung-siang, *Chinese Emigration to Borneo and the Eastern Passage* (王詠祥教授：華人移殖婆羅洲東航線攷), published in the *Chinese Daily News* in its New Year's Day special edition of 1974.

Ward, Barbara, 'A Hakka Kongsi in Borneo', *Journal of Oriental Studies*, Hong Kong, Vol. 1, No. 2, July 1959.

Magazine Commemorating the Fiftieth Anniversary of the Establishment of Foochow Settlement in Sibu (1901–1950) (砂勝越詩巫福州墾場五十周年紀念特刊), 1951.

Magazine Commemorating the Twenty-fifth Anniversary of

the Establishment of the Hokkien Free School, 1937
(福建義務學校廿五周年紀念特刊).

Sarawak Museum Journal.
Sarawak Tribune.
Chinese Daily News (中華日報).

Index

Abang Haji Mustapha, Datu Bandar, 122, 135n
Abdul Rahman Yaakub, Datuk Patinggi Haji, 125, 127
Abdul Razak, Tun, 127
Abell, Governor Sir Anthony, 118
Agriculture, 14-15, 21, 27, 28, 29, 43-4, 45, 46, 57-8, 76; cash crops, 15, 29, 51, 73, 104-5; Chinese settlements, 59-69, 75; food crops, 14, 15, 27, 29, 51, 72, 98
Akhmed, Sultan of Brunei, 4
Alli Kawi, 129
American Methodists, 61, 65, 66-7
Anglicans, 60
Anglican Church of Borneo, 89, 90
Antimony mining, 25, 27
Arrack, 29, 30, 40, 45, 50n, 63, 66, 73

Bampfylde, C. A., 8, 69
Bandar Kuching, 126, 128, 130
Banjermasin Sultanate, West Borneo, 8, 23
Baram, 49, 65; agricultural settlements, 67-8
Baring-Gould, S., 8, 69

Barisan Nasional Sarawak (Sarawak National Front), 121, 127-8, 129-31
Basel Mission in China, 59
Batavia (Jakarta), 22, 24
Batu Kawa, 59
Bau kongsi, 25, 26, 28-30, 31, 32-4, 72, 76, 103; Chinese Rebellion, 35, 40, 41; post-rebellion return of, 41
Belidah fort, 33
Benevolent Societies, 84
Berkat, Sultan of Brunei (Sharif Ali), 4
Binatang, 65, 88, 115
Bintulu, 67, 115
Borneo, early Chinese contacts with, 1-8; see also Sabah; Sarawak; West Borneo
Borneo Company, 30, 38n, 41
Boxer uprising, China, 62
Braddell, R., 1-2
Brewster, Revd William, 66
British Borneo Civil Administration Unit (BBCAU), 101
British colonial rule, 24, 27, 28, 29-30, 53, 100, 101-15; see also Brooke, Rajah

British North Borneo Company, 49

British War Funds, 95

Brooke, Anthony, 118

Brooke, Rajah Charles (ruled 1868–1917), 33, 44, 45, 47, 48, 49, 57, 58, 83; Chinese Rebellion and, 36, 51; attitude to Chinese, 41, 51, 53; Chinese immigration encouraged by, 51, 53-5, 75; and land settlement policies, 58, 59, 60, 62, 65, 66, 67, 68, 75; and education, 88-9; Agreement with Wong Nai Siong for immigration of Foochows (1900), 62-3, 136-9; and Agreement between Cantonese Company and (1901), 140-2

Brooke, Rajah Charles Vyner (ruled 1917–41), 68, 75; social measures introduced by, 78-9; new constitution proclaimed by (1941), 95-6; post-war return to Sarawak, 101; cedes Sarawak as colony to Britain, 101-2

Brooke, Rajah James (ruled 1841–68), 15, 25, 27, 28, 49, 51, 73, 77, 88, 96; land law of (1863), 41, 57; Chinese Rebellion against rule of, 15, 28, 34-8, 40-1; attitude to Bau kongsi, 28, 29-30; and to opium, 33-4; and changing view of Chinese, 41; death, 44

Brooketon coal mine, 54

Brotherhood of Eighteen, 18

Brunei, 22, 23, 25, 27, 68, 97, 123; early Chinese contacts with, 1-4, 7, 10; and Chinese population, 7-8; land ceded to Sarawak by, 49; 1962 Revolt, 121

BUMIPUTRA (Parti Bumiputra Bersatu), 121, 123, 125-7

Canton, 5, 34

Cantonese, 17, 46, 59, 65-6, 70n, 74, 75

Cantonese Company, Agreement between Charles Brooke and (1901), 140-2

Chai Chong Fea, 130

Chan Kay Soon, 43, 48

Chan Kho, 42, 43, 44, 45, 73

Chang Ah Chai, 18

Chao-Ann Association, 84

Chao-Ann community, 43, 45, 74

Chao Ju-kua, 2

Chater, W. J., 56-7

Cheng Ho, Imperial eunuch, 4-5, 6, 10-11n

Chia Chin Shin, 130

Chiang Cho Shiong, 65-6, 140

China, Mainland, 29; early contacts with Borneo, 1-8, 13; seafaring tradition, 5-6; early contacts with Sarawak, 9-10; village organization, 15, 17; Triad Society, 30-2; troubles with English merchants in Canton, 34; labour brokers in treaty ports, 53; recruited, free and sponsored immigrations into Sarawak from, 51-8; Christians and missionaries, 59, 61, 62; reform movement (1898), 61-2; Boxer uprising, 62; Sino-Japanese War, 95, 97, 107; Sarawak Chinese' preoccupation with events in, 104; Nationalists, 97, 112; Communist regime, 112, 132-3

China Relief Fund, 82, 95

Chinese Advisory Board, 112

Chinese Chamber of Commerce, 84, 96, 103, 105-6, 110, 112, 113, 115, 116n

Chinese coins, 9

Chinese Democratic Political Society, 112

Chinese immigration, 7, 8, 13-16; into Sarawak, 25-6, 27, 28, 48, 51, 53-7, 73; recruited labourers, 53-5; free, 55-7; sponsored, 57; agricultural settlements and, 59-69; Agreement between Charles Brooke and Wong Nai Siong for Foochows' immigration (1900), 136-9; and Agreement between Charles Brooke and Cantonese Company (1901), 140-2

Chinese merchants in Sarawak, 35, 40, 41-4, 45, 55, 72, 73, 75, 76, 77, 78, 79, 84

Chinese miners, 72; in West Borneo, 14, 15-17, 27-8; and in Sarawak, 27, 28, 29, 30; rebellion against Brooke's rule by, 15, 28, 34-8, 40; influence of Triad on, 32, 33

Chinese National Day, 113

Chinese newspapers, 106-9, 122

Chinese People's Association, 83

Chinese population in Sarawak: distribution (map), 52, 74; and growth, 68-9

Chinese Protectorate (later Secretariat for Chinese Affairs), 78

Chinese Rebellion (1857), 15, 28, 34-8, 40-1, 51, 103

Ch'ing dynasty, 6-7, 30, 61

Chong Kiun Kong, 128

Chow Chu-fei, 5

Christians, Christianity, 59-60, 61, 62, 65, 89; see also Missionaries

Chu Hung Wu, 3-4

Chua Kok Beng, Dr, 130

Chung Cheng School, Sibu, 88

Chung Hua Association, 112

Chung Hua School, Sibu, 87, 88

Chung Poon School, Kuching, 88

Clan or community associations, 17, 28, 80, 81-4, 100; schools, 84-8, 106

Clandestine Communist Organisation (CCO), 111, 119; see also SCO

Colonial Development and Welfare Fund, 104

Communal organization, 71, 80-4, 103; see also Education

Communists, 93, 111-12, 113, 119, 122, 126, 127, 132

Contract Chinese labour system, 53-4

Council Negri (State Council), 96, 102, 110, 114, 115, 116n, 124, 129, 131, 135n

Dayaks, 33, 58, 102, 118; members of political parties, 119, 121, 122, 123

De Groot, 14, 18, 20, 26n

Democratic Action Party (DAP), 129, 131

Dewan Undangan Negri, 131

Diamond mining, 27

District Councils, 110, 116n, 123

Divisional Councils, 110, 116n

Domestic animals (livestock), 21, 29, 60

Dutch, Dutch colonialism, 8, 13-14, 55; in West Borneo, 14, 16, 17, 22-5, 26n, 28, 31, 37; trade, 13, 22-3; kongsi wars, 23-5

Dutch East India Company, 8, 22, 23

Earl, G. W., 17

Economic power/organization, 71-6

Education, 21, 71, 82, 84-93, 100, 117; Chinese-medium schools, 84-8, 105-6, 113, 114; and English-medium missionary schools, 88-90, 105, 106; private tutoring, 84-5; social gulf between Chinese-educated and English-educated, 90-3; post-war colonial, 105-6; teacher-training colleges, 105; and foreign scholarships, 105; Malay vernacular, 106; Grant Code Regulations (1956), 106, 114; radical movement and changes (1950s), 113-15

Ellis, J. H., Chief Secretary, 117-18

Emergency Ordinances (1962), 121-2, 135n

English newspapers, 106-8

Fa Hsien, Buddhist monk, 1-2

Fan Tsuo, 1

Federation of Malaysia, Sarawak gains independence as member of (1963), 124, 125

Feng-shan Temple, Kuching, 81

Fifth Division of Sarawak, 49, 58, 68, 75

First Division of Sarawak, 49, 58, 59, 67, 75, 76, 79, 87, 88, 95n, 105

Foochow Association, 83

Foochow Kong Yan Society, 84

Foochows, 45-6, 59, 62, 75, 105; agricultural settlements, 60-1, 62-5, 67-8, 70n, 76, 89; schools, 87, 88; SCA members, 120, 121, 122; Agreement between Charles Brooke and Wong Nai Siong for immigration of (1900), 62-3, 136-9

Forest resources, 21

Fourth Division of Sarawak, 49, 67-8, 75

Gambier cultivation, 15, 29, 41, 43, 45, 46, 57-8, 70n, 72

Gambling, 29-30, 32, 40, 45, 66, 73, 102

General elections: 1963: 120, 124; 1970: 121, 125, 126; 1974: 121, 127-8; 1978: 128-30

Genghiz Khan, 3

Ghee Soon and Co., 44, 45

Gold mining, 8, 13, 14, 15, 18, 21, 23-4, 27, 28, 29-30, 38-9n, 41, 43, 45

Government, Chinese participation in, 123-30

Grant Code Regulations (1956), 106, 114

Great Java War, 24

Greater East Asia Co-prosperity Sphere, 98

Gunseibo (Japanese Military Administration), Kuching, 98

Hainanese, 17, 74, 81

Hakka Community Association, 84, 88

Hakkas, 15, 18, 43, 74, 75, 76, 79, 87, 105, 134n; kongsi system, 15, 17; Christian agricultural settlement, 59-60, 76; SUPP members, 119

Hall, D. G. E., 2

Harrisson, T., 23, 26n

Hashim, Rajah Muda, 27

Headmen see Kangchews

Helms, Ludwig, 36

Henghuas, 66-7, 74

Hiawang (Si Awang), King of P'oni, 5

Hock Long Co., 63

Hokkien Association, 83, 88

Hokkien Free School, 47, 48, 86, 87, 88, 115n

Hokkiens, 45, 46, 48, 75, 77, 81, 105, 119

Hoover, Revd James, 65, 67

Huichow dialect, 17

Hunt, J., 7

Hussein Onn, Datuk, 128, 130

Ibans, 36, 119, 123, 130

Indian labourers in Sarawak, 54

Indirect rule, 77, 83, 103

Indonesian communists, 122

Initiation ceremonies, 32

Iron foundries, 9-10

James Brooke, 36

Japanese occupation of Sarawak (1941-5), 75, 82, 87, 93, 95-101

Java, 2, 3, 7, 22, 26n, 53

Johnson, A. L., and Co., 53

Jugah anak Barieng, Temenggong, 123

Kai Wen School, Binatang, 88

Kalong Ningkan, Stephen, 123, 124-5

Kangchews (area headmen), 59, 63, 64, 66, 70n, 78, 85, 86, 103, 110

K'ang Yu-wei, 61

Kanowit, 65, 66, 88

Kapit, 65

Kapitans China, 78, 85, 103, 110, 134n

Kayans, 49, 130

Kaying (Five Common Clans) Association, 83, 88

Kempetai (military police), 98, 99

Kertanagara, King, 3

Khengchew (Hainanese) Association, 83, 88

Khi Ting Primary School, Kanowit, 88

Kho Peng Loong, 102, 115n

Kong Kwei En, 60

Kongsis, West Borneo, 15-21, 28, 31; Lan-fang, 17-21, 24-5; conflicts among, 24, 26, 28; Bau, 25, 26, 28-30, 32-4, 72, 76, 103; Ta-kong, 17, 19, 23, 24-5, 26, 28; wars with Dutch, 23-5; San-Tiou-Kow, 24, 25, 26, 28; 1857 Rebellion against James Brooke, 15, 28, 34-8, 40; influence of Triad refugees on, 31-2; post-rebellion return of, 41

Kong-Wei-Shiu Association, 83, 88

Kuang Hsi, Emperor, 61, 70n

Kublai Khan, 3

Kuching, 25, 40, 53, 54, 55, 59, 66, 74, 76, 77; Chinese rebels' occupation of (1857), 35-6; post-rebellion pioneers, 40-4; temples, 81; clan associations, 83-4; schools, 86, 87, 88, 90, 105, 106; Japanese occupation, 96, 97; newspapers, 106, 107, 108, 113; Nationalist Chinese consul in, 112; political parties, 119, 120; students' strikes and left-wing activity, 113-14

Kuching Chinese Chamber of Commerce, 84, 134n

Kuching Chinese community, 60

Kuching Municipal Council, 134n, 135n

Kung Min School, Kuching, 88

Kwangchow province, 13, 17

Kyodo-heis (local army corps), 98

Labour squads, 97, 98

Labuan, 54, 97

Lag Mandor, 14, 18-19

Lambir constituency, 130

Land Dayaks, 119, 123

Land Law (1863), 41, 57, 58

Land Rules (1933), 103

Lan-fang corporation, 21

Lan-fang kongsi, 12, 17-21, 23, 24-5
Larak, West Borneo, 13, 14
Lau Chek, 42
Law Kian Huat, 42, 43-4, 45, 56, 73
Lawas, 49, 68
Leadership, Chinese: 1841–1910: 44-8; structure, 71, 76-80; post-war struggle for, 111; *see also* Government; Political parties
Lee Cheng Tien, 47
Lee Soon Kheng, 46
Lek Chiang (Lek Ngee Seng), 63, 64-5, 70n
Liang dynasty, 2
Liew Shan-pang, 25, 26
Liew Syn Ted, 41, 50n
Liew Tai-irk, 24
Lim Boon Kheng, Dr, 62, 70n
Lim Eng Moh, 42
Limbang, 49, 68, 128
Ling Beng Siew, 121, 135n
Lo Fang-pai, 17, 18-20
Lo Foot Kee, 128, 130
Lo Hsiang-lin, 26n
Local authority elections, 117, 123, 134n
Local Authority Ordinance (1948), 110, 111, 134n
Low, Hugh, 7-8
Luichew dialect, 17
Luiyang (Luichew) Association, 84
Lundu, 51, 58
Lutong, 97
Luzon, 3

MACHINDA, 123
McDougall, Bishop Francis, 35, 36
Magellan, Ferdinand, 5
Majapahit kingdom, 3
Malacca, 6, 22

Malay National Union, 118
Malayan Chinese Association (MCA), 120
Malayan Communist Party, 111
Malays, 3, 58, 102, 119; Chinese Rebellion and, 35, 36; vernacular schools, 106; political parties, 122-3, 124
Malaysian Solidarity Convention (1965), 119
Manchus, 6-7, 30, 31
Mandarin language, 87
Maraja Kali, King of P'oni, 5
Marriage, 78-9
Matang, 54
Matusain, Sharif, 33
Melanaus, 2, 119
Mempawa, 14, 23
Methodists, 61, 65, 66-7, 89, 90
Min Teck School, Kuching, 87, 88
Ming dynasty, 3-4, 5, 6, 10, 30
Miri, 74, 114, 115, 129; oilfields, 67, 96, 97; schools, 86, 105; newspapers, 109
Missionaries, 59, 60, 61, 65, 66; schools, 88-90, 94n, 105, 106
Montrado, Borneo, 14, 23
Montrado kongsi, 12, 19
Mukah, 49

Nanking, 4, 5
Nanyang, 4, 6, 62
Newspapers: pre-war, 106, 107; post-war, 106-7, 108-9; proscription of left-wing, 113, 122
Noort, Oliver van, 22

O'Connor, Stanley J., 23, 26n
Ogotai Khan, 3
Omar Alamudin, Sultan of Pontianak, 14
Ong Ewe Hai, 42-3, 44, 45, 48, 73, 78

Ong Hap Leong, 115n
Ong Kee Hui, 118, 126, 128, 130, 134n
Ong Sum Ping, 4
Ong Tiang Swee, 43, 48, 62, 78, 96, 134n
Opium, 29, 30, 32, 40, 45, 63, 66, 73, 102; Rajah Brooke's monopoly of sale, 30, 33; Chinese use of, 33-4
Opium War, 33
Overseas Chinese, status of, 132-3
Oya, 49

Pamangkat, 24, 28
Pangkalan Tebang, 27
Pan-Malaysian Chinese General Chamber of Commerce, 116n
Parti Berasa, 129
Parti Berjaya, Sabah, 128
Parti Bumiputra Bersatu see BUMIPUTRA
Parti Negara Rakyat Sarawak (PNRS or PEACE), 129
Parti Negara Sarawak (PANAS), 122, 124, 135n
Parti PESAKA (Pesaka Anak Sarawak), 122, 123, 125, 127
Parti Ra'ayat Jati Sarawak (BARJASA), 122-3, 124
Parti Rakyat Jati Sarawak (PAJAR), 129, 130, 131
Paterson, Simons and Co., 54
Payne, Robert, 25, 26n
Peking Treaty (1860), 53
Pepper cultivation/trade, 8, 13, 14, 15, 23, 29, 40, 41, 43, 45, 46, 58, 66, 67, 70n, 72, 76, 104-5
Pigafetta, 7
PNRS or PEACE (Parti Negara Rakyat Sarawak) see Parti Negara Rakyat Sarawak

Political parties, Chinese, 113; formation of, 117-23; Chinese participation in coalition government, 123-31
P'oni see Brunei
Pontianak, 8, 14, 23, 29
Portuguese, 8, 22
Pottery, ceramics, 9, 10
Poyut, Baram, 68
Preservation of Public Security Regulations (1962), 121, 126
Pulau Satang, Sarawak, 9

Rejang settlements, 49, 51, 59, 60, 62, 64, 66, 67, 68, 75, 89, 102, 136-9
Rice (padi) cultivation, 59, 60, 62, 66, 104
Roman Catholic Mission, Kuching, 89, 90
Rubber cultivation, 72, 76, 104, 105
Runciman, Steven, 42
Rupell, English merchant, 36
Rural bazaar shopkeepers, 72, 76, 77, 85, 86, 94n
Rural settlers, 72, 76, 77

Sabah (North Borneo), 3, 4, 68, 97, 128, 129
Sadong coal mine, 54
Sago, 49; processing and refining, 41, 44, 73
St. John, Spenser, 7, 8
St Joseph's School, Kuching, 90, 105, 134n
St Mary's (Girls') School, Kuching, 105
St Teresa's (Girls') School, Kuching, 105
St Thomas's School, Kuching, 90, 105, 134n
Salamon, 19-20

Sambas, West Borneo, 13, 14, 18, 19, 22, 23, 25, 27, 29, 37, 41, 49
San-Tiou-Kow kongsi, 24, 25, 26, 28
Santoh, 23
Santubong excavations, Sarawak, 9-10
SAPO (Sarawak People's Organization), 129, 130, 131
Sarawak: early contacts between Chinese and, 9-10; Lan-fang kongsi, 17-21; Brooke becomes Rajah (1841), 27, 28; Chinese Rebellion (1857), 28, 34-8; Bau kongsi, 25, 26, 28-30, 32-8; Triad's influence, 31-2, 33; early Chinese pioneers, 40-4; and Chinese leadership, 44-8; extension of territory, 48-9; Chinese immigration, 25-6, 27, 28, 48, 51, 53-9, 74, 136-42; and agricultural settlements, 59-69; economic power, 71-6; leadership structure, 71, 76-80; communal organization, 80-4; and education, 84-92; Japanese occupation (1941-5), 75, 82, 83, 95-101; new Constitution (1941), 95-6; amended Constitution (1957), 124; BBCAU administration, 101; early post-war years and colonial rule, 101-15; ceded by Rajah to Britain (1946), 101-2; Local Authority Ordinance (1948), 110; formation of political parties, 117-23; Chinese participation in government, 123-30; emergency regulations (1962), 121; Independence (1963), 124; see also West Borneo
Sarawak Alliance, 122, 124
Sarawak Chinese Association (SCA), 119-21, 122, 124, 125
Sarawak Communist Organisation (SCO), 111, 122, 126, 127; see also CCO
Sarawak Dayak Association, 118
Sarawak Education Council, 114
Sarawak Gazette, 60, 106, 107, 115-16n
Sarawak National Front see Barisan Nasional Sarawak
Sarawak National Party (SNAP), 122, 123, 124, 125, 127-8, 130
Sarawak United People's Party (SUPP), 118-20, 121-2, 124, 125-8, 129
Sarikei, 65, 88, 114, 117
Sarikei Chinese Chamber of Commerce, 115
Schlegedate, 14
Sebauh (Bintulu), 65, 68
Second Division of Sarawak, 49, 67, 75
Second World War, 83, 95-101, 110-11
Seminis, 24
Seria, 96, 97
Seventh Day Adventist Mission, 89
Shan Hsin Gold Lake (gold mine), 18-19
Shang-ti Temple, Kuching, 81
Sibu, 64, 65, 66, 67, 70n, 75, 115; schools, 86, 87, 88, 105, 114; Japanese occupation, 96; newspapers, 106, 107, 109; SBA members, 120, 121
Sim Ah Nio, 44
Sim Kheng Hong, 125-6, 128
Simanggang, 42
Sin Ann dialect, 17
Singapore, 29, 31, 40, 57, 62; Chinese uprising (1857), 34; Sarawak trade with, 41, 42-3, 72; Chinese immigration into Sara-

wak via, 53-4, 55, 62-3; Japanese occupation, 97
Singkawang airfield, 97
Sinkehs (new immigrants), 56
Sino-Japanese War, 95, 97, 107
Social and political organization, Chinese: kongsi system, 15-21, 76; leadership structure, 76-80; communal organization, 80-4; education, 84-92
Society for the Propagation of the Gospel, 89
Song, 65
Song Kheng Hai, 47
Spanish, 8, 22
Sri Aman agreement (1974), 127
State Council *see* Council Negri
State elections (1979), 131; *see also* General elections
Straits Settlements, 7, 54, 55
Students' strikes, Kuching, 113-14, 118
Su P'e, General, 3
Sui dynasty, 2
Sukarno, President of Indonesia, 122
Sulu islands, 3, 4
Sumatra (Palembang), 2, 3, 4, 23
Sun Yat Sen, Dr, 46, 47, 83
Sung dynasty, 2
Sungei Buah, 10
Sungei Ja'ong trade centre, 9, 10
Sungei Lanang, 66
Sungei Maong, 59
Sungei Merah (Sin Che San), 64, 66
Swatow, 56
Sze Mei School, Sarikei, 88
sze-su (private tutoring), 85
Szetu Mei Thong, Raymond, 130

T'ai Tung School, Kuching, 88
T'aipu Clan Association, 83, 88

Ta-kong kongsi, 17, 19, 23, 24-5, 26, 28, 29
Tamerlane, Emperor, 4
Tan, Sultan of Sulu, 4
Tan, William, 120-1, 134-5n
Tan Boh Seng, 46-7, 134n
Tan Sum Guan, 115n
T'ang dynasty, 1, 2, 9
Tang Kung Suk, 46, 65-6, 140
Tanjong Kubu cemetery, 9
Tanjong Sipang, 9
Tanjong Tegok cemetery, 9
Tap'u Hakkas, 18
Taxation, 23, 29, 30, 34
Tea, 29, 54
Telok Sabang, 10
Temples, 80-1; used as classrooms, 84
Teo Chong Loh, 46
Teo Kui Seng, 124
Teochew Association, 83, 88
Teochews, 17, 43, 44, 45, 46, 56, 75, 81, 87, 120, 122, 134n
Third Division of Sarawak, 49, 50n, 59, 67, 75, 76, 87, 88, 94n, 105, 121
T'ien, Dr J. K., 93n
T'ien Hor Temple, Kuching, 81
Timber/sawmilling industry, 68, 105
Ting Kuang Tow, Revd, 70n
Tobacco, 29, 54
Trade and commerce, 7-8, 9-10, 13, 14, 22-3, 29, 30, 32, 41, 42-3, 44, 45, 47, 55, 68, 72-3, 75, 104-5
Trade licensing fees, 114, 117
Treaty of Nanking (1842), 33, 61
Treaty of Peking (1860), 7, 13
Triad Society, 30-2, 33, 34, 37
Trusan, 49, 68
Tuanku Haji Bujang, Datu, 122
T'ung Cher, Emperor, 70n

Tze Shuen Sung, 115n
Tzu Hsi, Dowager Empress, 61, 69-70n

UMAT (United Malaysia Timur Organization), 129, 131
UMNO (West Malaysia), 123
Upper Sarawak, 15, 24, 25-6, 27, 89; see also Sarawak
Urban businessmen/merchants, 72, 73, 75, 76, 77, 78, 79, 84, 104, 105
USNO, 128

Vegetable gardening, 60, 62, 66, 72
Vijaya, King, 3

Ward, Barbara, 15
Wee Kheng Chiang, 96, 134n
West Borneo, 22, 40; early Chinese trade with, 8; Lan-fang and Montrado kongsis, 12, 17-21; social and political organization, 13-18; early settlement, 13-14, 15-16;

kongsis, 15-21, 22, 29; kongsi wars and Dutch conquest, 22-5; Dutch colonial rule, 28, 37; migrations into Sarawak from, 25-6, 28, 31; see also Sarawak
Wong Kim Min, James, 124, 127-8
Wong Nai Siong, 45-6, 60-1, 62-5, 89; Agreement with Charles Brooke for immigration of Foochows (1900), 62-3, 136-9
Wong Soon Kai, Dr, 128
Woodhead Report, 114, 115

Yan dynasty, 3, 9
Yap Hsiang Yun, 17-18
Yeo Ban Hock, 47
Yik Kuan School, Kuching, 88
Yong Kuet Tze, Stephen, 118, 125, 128, 130, 131, 134n
Yueh Kwang School, Kuching, 87, 88
Yung Lo, Emperor of China, 4, 6, 10n

TH CHINA SEA

Mukah

Sibu

Sarikei • Kanovi

1861

Kuching
1841

1853 Simanggang